T0339668

Cambridge Elements ≡

Elements in Global China

edited by
Ching Kwan Lee
University of California-Los Angeles

CHINESE SOFT POWER

Maria Repnikova
Georgia State University

CAMBRIDGE
UNIVERSITY PRESS

University Printing House, Cambridge CB2 8BS, United Kingdom

One Liberty Plaza, 20th Floor, New York, NY 10006, USA

477 Williamstown Road, Port Melbourne, VIC 3207, Australia

314–321, 3rd Floor, Plot 3, Splendor Forum, Jasola District Centre,
New Delhi – 110025, India

103 Penang Road, #05–06/07, Visioncrest Commercial, Singapore 238467

Cambridge University Press is part of the University of Cambridge.

It furthers the University's mission by disseminating knowledge in the pursuit of education, learning, and research at the highest international levels of excellence.

www.cambridge.org
Information on this title: www.cambridge.org/9781108792684
DOI: 10.1017/9781108874700

© Maria Repnikova 2022

First published 2022

A catalogue record for this publication is available from the British Library.

ISBN 978-1-108-79268-4 Paperback
ISSN 2632-7341 (online)
ISSN 2632-7333 (print)

Chinese Soft Power

Elements in Global China

DOI: 10.1017/9781108874700
First published online: February 2022

Maria Repnikova
Georgia State University
Author for correspondence: Maria Repnikova, mrepnikova@gsu.edu

Abstract: This Element presents an overarching analysis of Chinese visions and practices of soft power. The analysis introduces Chinese theorization of soft power, as well as its practical implementation across global contexts. The key channels or mechanisms of China's soft power examined are the Confucius Institutes, international communication, education and training exchanges, and public diplomacy spectacles. The Element concludes with new directions for the field, drawing on the author's research on Chinese soft power in Ethiopia.

Keywords: China, Chinese influence, external propaganda, global China, public diplomacy, soft power

ISBNs: 9781108792684 (PB), 9781108874700 (OC)
ISSNs: 2632-7341 (online), 2632-7333 (print)

Contents

1 Rethinking Soft Power: The Views from China

Western media articles and policy reports relentlessly depict China's soft power efforts as futile or ineffective given its authoritarian system. More recently, some of China's soft power instruments, such as the Confucius Institutes (CIs) and state-owned media operations, have been recategorized as "sharp power" aimed at illicit control over public opinion. These critiques, however, have not deterred China's efforts. Following the accusations of coronavirus cover-ups in Wuhan, for instance, the party-state has furiously deployed a multitude of strategies, from media publicity to vaccine diplomacy, to transform its image from a troublemaker into that of a responsible leader and a global pandemic savior. This past June, President Xi Jinping has called for a presentation of a more "loveable" image of China that would strike the balance between confidence and humility as a way to win friends (BBC News 2021). The effectiveness of these efforts is yet to be comprehensively evaluated, but the persistent emphasis on soft power is noteworthy.

This Element delves into the ongoing efforts of the Chinese government to improve its soft power by illuminating the official visions as well as the workings of the key mechanisms, from CIs to media, to educational exchanges, to large-scale diplomatic events. It reveals the expansive and fluid interpretation and practice of soft power in China, whereby material resources and motivations tend to intermingle with political and cultural ones, and the target audience includes both domestic and international publics. Rather than definitively proclaim Chinese soft power as either a success or a failure, this Element presents the complex and often contradictory soft power performance. Chinese initiatives are at once ambitious and deliberately adaptive to local contexts; yet, they remain contested and perceived with mixed credibility, especially by external audiences. This section starts with the conceptual discussion, explaining how the very idea of soft power, originally conceived by Joseph Nye, has been readapted in the Chinese context.

Soft Power Travels to China

Joseph Nye, the US official and academic, coined the concept of "soft power" in 1990, at the tail end of the Cold War and right before the collapse of the Soviet Union. Nye argued that soft or co-optive power is at play when "one country gets other countries to want what it wants" and contrasted it with command or hard power of a country "ordering others to do what it wants" (Nye 1990, p. 166). More than a decade later, in his 2004 book, Nye elaborated on the distinction between hard and soft power. He articulated hard power as drawing on inducements (economic channels) and coercion (military threats), with soft power relying on attraction (Nye 2004).

Specifically, Nye underscored American culture, political ideals and values, and foreign policy as the key pillars of soft power. In many ways, soft power is a prescriptive idea, a recipe for a more effective US foreign policy. Soft power alone cannot accomplish all outcomes, and later Nye also presented the idea of "smart power," whereby hard and soft power are strategically and skillfully coordinated to achieve desired outcomes (Nye 2009). In the past two decades, the idea of soft power became a catchword for different facets of public diplomacy and nation branding. The concept has also been critiqued for its ambiguity that challenges its practical implementation and empirical measurement (Roselle et al. 2014), as well as for its contradictory and US-centric treatment of attraction (Mattern 2005).

The fluidity of the concept of "soft power," ironically, has also made it readily adaptable to other global contexts. China, in particular, has exhibited relentless curiosity and obsession with soft power. The term first emerged in Chinese leadership discourse in 2007, when President Hu Jintao mentioned the importance of strengthening China's cultural soft power (*wenhua ruan-shili* 文化软实力) at the 17th Party Congress. Xi Jinping has elevated the significance of soft power by invoking it in more speeches, including at the Third Plenary Session of the 18th Central Committee, the 19th Party Congress, as well as the 2018 major address on propaganda and ideology, among other high-level meetings. Xi emphasizes the importance of soft power for both domestic and international contexts. Domestically, Xi draws the connection between cultural soft power and China's development, framing cultural power as being on par with hard power: "The course of development for any big country throughout history includes the improvement of hard power like economic aggregate and military strength as well as the enhancement of soft power such as values, ideologies, and culture" (CPC News 2019). In his speeches, Xi also emphasizes the external dimension, including the importance of constructing international discourse power, especially vis-à-vis the West, and urging journalists to "tell the China story well" (Xinhua News Agency 2016). Much of Xi's rhetoric is motivational rather than analytical, taking the form of general directives for officials, experts, and journalists to improve China's soft power.

The official endorsements over the past two decades, and especially under Xi Jinping, have inspired a mass production of policy and academic writings on soft power. A search of the keyword "soft power" (*ruan shili* 软实力) in China's national academic database (CNKI) has located more than 7,000 academic articles.[1] This section introduces Chinese debates on soft power, drawing on about forty-five influential Chinese writings over the past two decades that were identified from major academic review pieces (Li 2008; Shu 2017; Wang & Guo 2012), the initial review of editorials on soft power published in *People's Daily* and *Qiushi* magazine,[2] and selective Western analyses that synthesize Chinese debates. What follows is the analysis of how Chinese experts conceptualize soft power, how they understand China's motivations for investing in it, as well as China's challenges and strategies for improving soft power. It is notable in these discussions that soft power in Chinese understanding is a more inclusive but also a more ambivalent concept than what Joseph Nye originally conceived. Chinese writings question the need for boundaries between hard and soft power and the very idea of attraction as separate from other inducements. They also debate key sources of Chinese soft power, from culture to political capacity to China's developmental model. In addition, unlike the external focus of soft power in the West, Chinese objectives behind soft power intermingle between external and domestic frontiers, with domestic publics being as much a target of soft power initiatives as international audiences.

Conceptual Debates: What Counts as Soft Power in China?

Many Chinese writings on soft power start out by quoting Nye's ideas but argue in favor of localizing or appropriating this concept for the Chinese context. In a widely cited media article published in 2005, for instance, Professor Pang Zhongying (Pang 2005) at Nankai University cautioned against China arbitrarily adopting Nye's concept conceived for American audiences. Chinese experts actively critique and reinterpret Nye's ideas, as evident in discussions about distinctions between hard (*ying shili* 硬实力) and soft (*ruan shili* 软实力) power, as well as in debates about key sources of soft power.

As for engaging with separation of hard and soft power, some Chinese writings propose more flexible frameworks. Li Mingjiang (Li 2009), for instance, argues that distinctions should be made about how power is practiced rather than the resources deployed. In his view, even military resources used "softly" (i.e., for the purposes of peacekeeping rather than war) can contribute to soft power. Others envision power as a continuum, with hard power drawing on coercion placed on one end of the spectrum, soft power or voluntary

---

[1] More than 17,000 article titles with the words "soft power" in the title came up in the title search.

[2] By focusing on scholars published and cited in *People's Daily* and *Qiushi*, I have selected the more influential voices that are likely to have wider reach with Chinese officials and public.

interactions positioned on the other, and bargaining power achieved through dialogue placed in between the two extremes (Zheng & Zhang 2007).

Hard power is also understood by many Chinese scholars as symbiotic with or as the foundation of soft power – something in part inferred from studying the experience of the West. Two communication scholars, for instance, write that "soft power of Western media was built on the foundation of hundreds of years of accumulation of hard power by the West" (Hu & Wang 2016, p. 18). Zhao Kejin (2014), an expert on China's public diplomacy at the Carnegie-Tsinghua Center, further draws linkages between economic and cultural power in the United States by noting that commercial products, like Coke, can also evolve into cultural symbols. China's continuing economic growth, in turn, is presented as a prerequisite for soft power (Huang & Ding 2010), China's ideas about economic governance as part of the broader concept of Chinese culture (Guo 2016), and China's foreign aid as one of the tools to spread soft power globally (Zhao 2007). This vision of an interactive relationship between soft and hard power in many ways mirrors Nye's idea of smart power. An important distinction, however, is that as Chinese writings question the need to separate hard and soft power, they also implicitly reject the possibility of pure attraction, embedded in Nye's notion of soft power.

The more ambiguous conception of soft power in Chinese narratives is also evident in the discussions of key sources of China's soft power. On the surface, it appears that culture is at the heart of the Chinese soft power conception, but culture itself is understood as a very open-ended concept that has political and ideological connotations. Alternative schools of thought, moreover, emphasize China's political capability and development model as the driving sources of its soft power.

As for the importance of culture, the majority of Chinese experts subscribe to the "cultural school" (*wenhua pai* 文化派) that places culture at the core of soft power. The prominence of the cultural school is evident in the emergence and popularization of the concept of "cultural soft power" (which has since become synonymous with soft power), and its numerous invocations by top leadership, starting with Hu Jintao and continuing with Xi. A new journal published by Wuhan University is even titled *Cultural Soft Power* (*wenhua ruanshili* 文化软实力), reflecting the urgency of this research agenda.

Yet, a closer look at the analysis of writings on cultural soft power reveals that culture is treated as an eclectic and fluid concept that encompasses Chinese traditional culture, moral principles, and political ideology. Chinese scholars refer to traditional culture – a product of China's 5,000-year history – as the heart of soft power. Traditional culture tends to be associated with moral principles rooted in China's philosophical traditions. These writings claim that the very idea of soft power has been part of Chinese culture for thousands of years, referencing China's classical works. Some invoke Confucian teachings of leading by example and Sun Tzu's military writings that emphasize winning the minds and resolving disputes through wisdom rather than through hard power (Ding 2010). Others refer to the Daoist teaching of "using softness to overcome hardness" (*yirou kegang*以柔克刚) as capturing the ideas of soft power (Shu 2017) and go as far as to claim that the secret to China's long civilization is its early grasp and practice of soft power (Feng 2016). The moral values associated with Chinese culture in these writings include respect for community, integrity, harmony, and accommodation of differences (*he er butong*和而不同). These values are presented as both inherent and aspirational, as scholars lament Chinese society's losing its way with the pursuit of money and pleasure. China's morally rooted cultural soft power is also contrasted with the morally vacuous soft power of the United States, which pursues hegemonic cultural domination or "American exceptionalism" (Wang 2016). One of China's core tasks, therefore, is to explain China's moral values to the world and to offer an attractive alternative to the United States.

This defense of morality is fused with ideological discussions of culture as "Socialism with Chinese Characteristics" (and "Core Socialist Values") and public unity around the Chinese Communist Party's ideology and principles. The party is presented as the carrier of China's traditional values and civilization, and of national spirit and morale (*minzu shiqi*民族士气) (Wang 2018). Chinese culture is also described as the societal glue that creates national cohesion by placing patriotism at the heart of development (Yan & Zhao 2016). Overall, Chinese writings treat culture as an all-encompassing invisible force responsible for creating a more morally grounded and politically unified Chinese polity.

A contrasting perspective to the cultural school, advocated by the Tsinghua University professor and public intellectual Yan Xuetong (2007), treats politics as the essence of China's soft power. According to Yan, soft power can be accomplished without cultural power, but it requires political power to mobilize domestically and internationally. He notes the collapse of the Roman Empire, the Qing dynasty, and the British Empire as examples of vast cultural power but weak political mobilization. Yan understands political power as the ability to operationalize resources, including culture, to the nation's advantage.

Yan's article stirred some controversy, with leading scholars defending the essence of culture for China's soft power. Lu Gang (2007), the head of Russia and Central Asia Research at the Shanghai Institute of International Affairs, for instance, noted that despite being relatively successful at garnering political prestige, China's soft power is still inadequate, bringing back the importance of cultural power. The debate between the cultural and the political schools, however, is somewhat artificial. Whereas the cultural camp sees China's moral and political values as the heart of soft power, the political camp sees culture as one of China's resources to be effectively mobilized, especially in the international arena. Moreover, both see culture and politics as entwined, with culture manifesting political ideology and helping mobilize the public in support of China's policies.

Another, alternative reconceptualization of soft power in the Chinese context emphasizes China's development model or experience as one of the core features, especially when it comes to China's appeal in the developing world. Some Chinese scholars see China as offering a competitive vision to the Washington Consensus – something they describe as the "China model" (*zhongguo moshi* 中国模式) or "Chinese development model" (*zhongguo fazhan moshi* 中国发展模式). The key features include prioritization of economic development, flexibility and experimentation, strong leadership of the state in guiding and correcting the reform process, and the combination of active participation in globalization and autonomy (Men 2007; Yu & Zhuang 2004). Even when not referencing a model, some studies invoke China's successful economic practices, such as enterprise innovation and company management experiences, as part of its soft power appeal (Jiang & Ye 2009).

At the same time, there is still much debate as to the specificity and universality of the China model, with some experts suggesting that selective countries in the Global South have already adopted some of China's practices of industrialization, infrastructure development, and manufacturing (Cheng 2018), and others cautioning that China should not expect developing countries to entirely copy its experience and instead should anticipate China sparking inspiration to practice self-determination (Luo 2019).

The cultural, political, and developmental perspectives are fluid and interactive in Chinese analyses of soft power, with many writings featuring some interplay of all three. Wang Yiwei (2016), a professor at the School of International Studies at Renmin University of China, for instance, argues that Chinese soft power draws on Chinese culture, the Chinese model in-the-making, and the Chinese Dream that demonstrates Chinese values and identity to the world. Others argue that soft power consists of short-term attractiveness generated through perceptions of a country's technology, arts, citizens' behavior, and state abilities, as well as the attractiveness of the country's political system and political principles and values (Jiang & Ye 2009). Some propose distinguishing between institutional power and the state's capacity to create new institutions, identifying power or influence through recognition of one's leadership and assimilating power that includes attractiveness of ideology, culture, and social system (Gong 2007, cited in Li 2008).

Motivations for Soft Power: The Hybrid of Domestic and International

As already noted, Nye's conception of soft power was motivated by his reckoning with the decline in US global influence in the post–Cold War world. Chinese scholars and policymakers, in contrast, envision soft power as pertinent for achieving China's international objective of peaceful rise, as well as for accomplishing the domestic goal of political stability. China is further portrayed as struggling to safeguard its legitimacy internationally and domestically from challenges presented by the West (and the United States in particular).

As for external motivations, an apparent sense of urgency is conveyed in Chinese writings about rectifying the imbalance between China's economic rise and its voice in the international system. Soft power is presented as an essential if not the main symbol of international status that determines China's position as a great power. Yu Guoming, China's renowned communication scholar at Renmin University, argues as follows: "The strength of our voice does not match our position in the world. That affects the extent to which China is accepted by the world. If our voice does not match our role, however strong we are, we remain a crippled giant" (Guo & Lye 2011, cited in Zhao 2013, p. 22). Many writings further explain China's weak soft power with the "China threat" narrative promoted by the West. Zhao Kejin (2005), deputy director of the Institute of International Relations at Tsinghua University, envisions the role of public diplomacy as that of creating a "soft landing" in the international system by mitigating global fears of China's rise driven by Western narratives. Other scholars promote a more aggressive response to Western narratives (Liu 2017a; Lynch 2020).

International acceptance is also interlinked with China's domestic development in these writings. Luo Jianbo (2017), a professor of diplomacy at the Central Party School, argues that one of the core goals of China's diplomacy should be creating a favorable external environment for China's national rejuvenation. Others argue that the acceptance of China by the international community carries an important signal to China's domestic public about the realization of China's rise and the China Dream (Lynch 2020).

Some writings articulate the linkages between soft power and domestic legitimacy in more explicit terms. Namely, the concept of "cultural confidence" (*wenhua zixin* 文化自信) features strongly in some discussions of soft power, especially in the Xi era. Explained by Xi as the importance of Chinese people having confidence in their own culture and in China's path of development (Klimeš 2018), cultural confidence is seen as both a prerequisite for and the desired outcome of soft power. On the one hand, it is essential for enhancing China's attractiveness on the world stage; on the other, China's global attractiveness can boost domestic public appreciation for the uniqueness of Chinese culture, and implicitly for China's political system. Whereas Hu Jintao promoted a more neutral idea of cultural diplomacy, Xi's advocacy for cultural confidence celebrates the distinctiveness of China's cultural and moral values, indirectly discrediting external criticisms of China as not adhering to Western values and practices.

Some studies even envision soft power as a shield against Western cultural intrusion – something captured in another popular political concept of the Xi era, "cultural security" (*wenhua anquan* 文化安全). "Immunity" (*mianyili* 免疫力), a medical term, appears in discussions of the importance for China to build up resistance against Western cultural infiltration indirectly (Yan & Zhao 2016). The fear of destabilizing effects is justified through the examples of Western (and especially American) culture as inflaming the collapse of the Soviet Union, the Arab Spring, and other pro-democracy uprisings (Yan & Zhao 2016). Some writings go as far as to suggest that if soft power deteriorates, the country will face high risks of collapse and external subversion (Zhang 2015).

Throughout the discussions on motivations for soft power, it is evident that Chinese scholars largely respond to what they perceive as threats emanating from the West – the "West" often used as a synonym for the United States. Much of this rhetoric appears to stem from a perception of China's inadequacy when it comes to its soft power, especially in comparison with the West, as explained in the following section.

Insecurities and Ambitions

"The West is strong, China is weak" – a phrase invoked in many works – captures the popular thesis that China still lags behind the West in global cultural attractiveness. With rare exceptions (Yan & Xu 2008), most writings focus on China's challenges and offer constructive solutions for improving its image. The key challenges outlined are China's weak competitiveness in cultural and media industries – something linked to both Western dominance and China's internal shortcomings.[3]

---

[3] These challenges are also underscored in Mingjiang Li's review article on soft power. Interestingly, thirteen years after the publication of his essay, Chinese scholars underscore the same core challenges.

As for cultural competitiveness, Western cultural hegemony is highlighted as the key barrier. One study (Luo 2013), for instance, cites a statistic from 2011 that the United States occupies 43 percent of the global cultural market and China only captures 4 percent. Others point to China's failure to effectively deploy its abundant cultural resources for soft power. In particular, China's cultural advantage is seen as derived from the "hardware" of cheap production rather than from the "software" of cultural products and ideas (Luo 2013), and China's overreliance on state actors and traditional culture is deemed ineffective (Zhao 2014).

Weak media or communication power is another concern. Here again, part of the explanation is that of pervasive (and harmful) Western influence. China's communication experts write that Western news agencies produce the majority of global news content (Yao 2007, cited in Li 2008), including the most cited stories on China (Xu 2014). In comparison, despite being the world's largest media organization, Xinhua is unable to match the global influence of major Western media (Xu 2014).

At the same time, Chinese writings also openly admit the inadequacy of China's story-telling practices, citing President Xi himself as saying that "China lacks effective storytelling techniques to justify its position/status, and even if it tells stories to the world, it does not have the channels to spread its stories or amplify their influence" (Hu & Wang 2016, p. 19).

As anticipated from China's long tradition of expressing constructive criticism in intellectual writings (Repnikova 2017), Chinese writings on soft power tend to conclude their discussions of challenges with extensive lists of suggestions, most of them focused on domestic or internal adjustments. As for cultural competitiveness, they advocate strengthening China's cultural industry (Shen 2017; Tong 2008), better promoting China's core socialist values (Shu 2017), and incorporating modern or contemporary culture into cultural initiatives (Zhao 2014). Chinese experts also propose to strengthen media power by practicing more comprehensive storytelling (Hu & Wang 2016). Some writings even delicately advocate for reform of the news and communication system that would allow for more creativity for media outlets (Han 2006) and more room for journalists to engage with their audiences (Xu 2013). The challenges and especially the suggestions for improvement are discussed in broad strokes. This may in part be due to the political sensitivity of this topic. Similarly to Chinese journalists who tend to promote suggestions agreeable to the central state (Repnikova 2017), Chinese scholars of soft power conclude their analyses with an eclectic mix of recommendations that are diverse and broad enough to satisfy any official reader.

Conclusion: China's Distinctive Visions of Soft Power

Chinese writings echo Nye's agenda of enhancing power via global attractiveness. Yet, Chinese experts conceive of soft power as at once a more flexible and a more pressing idea. Whereas Nye clearly distinguishes between hard and soft power, Chinese writings often merge the two, with attraction seen as inseparable from other inducements. Whereas Nye presents soft power sources as foreign policy, values, and culture, Chinese writings present it as an eclectic mix of features, ranging from ideology to values to ancient history, national spirit, governance practices, and economic might. Whereas US studies tend to focus on external or foreign policy benefits, Chinese writings emphasize as much external as domestic implications. The domestic reasoning is especially distinctive. It conveys a sense of urgency in promoting soft power to ensure that Chinese culture can resist competing forces from the West. In theorizing about soft power, Chinese academic and policy writings tend to converge with and reinforce Xi's ideas, especially when it comes to a mix of domestic and external orientation of soft power, the importance of socialist values and ideology as part of Chinese culture, and the emphasis on China's lagging behind the West.

Some of these distinctive visions for Chinese soft power are illustrated in China's recent handling of its image during the coronavirus pandemic. In particular, we saw a fusion of soft and hard power, as the Chinese government at once mobilized external propaganda to publicize the stories of China's victory over the virus and disseminated material benefits or gifts via "mask diplomacy" and now also vaccine diplomacy especially in the developing world. Both soft and hard channels manifest the core features of Chinese culture, including the unified national spirit and China's principle of peaceful coexistence or "win-win" when it comes to diplomacy. The blending of external and domestic motivations in soft power promotion was also apparent during the pandemic. The story of China as a global savior was conveyed as much to external as to domestic audiences – a message that Chinese netizens have picked up with enthusiasm and pride.

The following sections proceed to examine how Chinese soft power visions play out in more detail by analyzing China's core soft power channels: Chinese language and culture institutes (Confucius Institutes), external communication, educational exchanges, and large-scale public diplomacy events. This Element does not claim to cover all facets of China's soft power engagements, but rather it focuses on the instruments that have featured highly in both Chinese and global debates. These channels or instruments are also not unique to China and make up the arsenal of public diplomacy of most nations.

2 The Controversies of Confucius Institutes

This section engages with Confucius Institutes (CIs) – arguably China's most contentious soft power mechanism. Since the opening of the first Confucius Institute in 2004 in Seoul, South Korea, this initiative has expanded rapidly. According to official sources, as of June 1, 2020, there are 541 Confucius Institutes and 1,170 Confucius Classrooms (CCs) in 162 countries/regions. In 2019 alone, 27 new Confucius Institutes and 66 Confucius Classrooms were opened, some of them in countries launching these initiatives for the first time (Xinhua News Agency 2019).

This rapid expansion has recently encountered some pushback, especially in Western democratic societies. In the United States, in August 2020, the US Department of State designated the Confucius Institute US Center (the de facto headquarters of all CIs and CCs) as a foreign mission of the People's Republic of China. The US Senate has since passed a measure that requires all universities to institute full oversight over CIs or else risk cuts in federal funding. As of March 2021, 74 CIs in the United States have either shut down or plan to do so (National Association of Scholars 2021). Deliberate closures of CIs have also taken place in New Zealand, Australia, and across Europe.

Confucius Institutes have been perceived with particular sensitivity in contrast to China's other soft power instruments in part because of their distinctive operations and management structure. Confucius Institutes are integrated into and cosponsored by host universities and as such are directly embedded into local institutions. Until recently, they have also been directly managed by Hanban, the Office of Chinese Language Council International, that is affiliated with the Chinese Ministry of Education and thus directly associated with the Chinese Communist Party. In his influential essay, Marshall Sahlins (2018), the late professor emeritus of anthropology at the University of Chicago, described CIs as the "academic malware" and "peripheral propaganda branches of the Chinese party-state." Other than fearing indoctrination of students, host universities may be wary of appearing as complicit in aiding the agenda of Beijing, especially in the current political climate. These concerns are most prevalent in the West, but they also linger in countries in the Global South, as will be explained further in this section. The discussion now proceeds to examining the missions of CIs, followed by their operations and observed effects, including political and practical challenges. Much of the analysis draws on documents and perspectives on CIs when under Hanban's management. In 2020, the operation of CIs was handed over to the newly established Chinese International Education Foundation, a nongovernmental organization initiated by a group of universities, companies, and cultural organizations; for now, there

Figure 1 Confucius Institute in Addis Ababa (Maria Repnikova)

are few publicly available details about whether and how the CI initiative will shift under this new foundation. As of June 2021, no CIs or CCs have closed as part of the changes in the organizational structure.

The Missions of CIs: Between Culture and Politics

There is an intriguing gap in how the mission of CIs is articulated by the Chinese participants and how it is perceived by outside observers, scholars, and recipients of this initiative. Hanban, the Office of Chinese Language Council International, that until last year was known as the Confucius Institute Headquarters, has promoted a depoliticized vision of cultural exchange. The Confucius Institutes Charter broadly characterized its mission as adapting to the global need of Chinese-language learning, enhancing understanding of Chinese culture, encouraging cultural exchange, and developing friendly relations with foreign nations. The last director general of Hanban, Xu Lin, revoked the political mission of CIs and, instead, underscored the aim of helping China be understood by the world (Hartig 2014). Most recently, Yang Wei, the chairman of the Chinese International Education Foundation (CIEF) that has managed CIs since 2020, has further distanced the mission of CIs from that of soft power by describing the Chinese International Education Foundation as philanthropic, contributing to cultural and educational exchange. Chinese education administrators and CI directors similarly tend to regard the mission of soft power with suspicion. Some differentiate between cultural diplomacy and cultural exchange, and others contrast what they perceive as cultural imposition embedded in the idea of soft power with what they aspire to as peaceful academic exchange (Hartig 2014).

Whereas Chinese officials tend to stress cultural and educational missions, external observers and experts tend to interpret CI objectives as political. The highest concentration of CIs in countries most resistant to China's rise, including the United States and the United Kingdom, signals the agenda of correcting prevailing misconceptions about China (Liu 2019). The fact that up until recently the management structure of CIs, whereby Hanban was affiliated with China's Ministry of Education, has also been interpreted as evidence of a political mission (Lahtinen 2015).

Views differ, however, as to what this political mission entails beyond the notion of improving China's image. The more balanced discussions tend to see the mission of CIs as that of influencing "global cultural discourse" rather than "forcing Chinese political doctrine upon the rest of the world" (Kluver 2017, p. 390). Some see CIs as similar to other international cultural institutes. Michael Spence, the vice-chancellor at the University of Sydney, for instance, argued that "the Confucius Institute is like the Alliance Francaise or Goethe-Institut. It teaches Chinese language and culture. . . . This is not people sitting around reading the Little Red Book" (Bonyhady & Baker 2019).

Yet, an increasingly popular view is that CIs are part of China's "sharp power" arsenal aimed at indoctrination and censorship rather than at open cultural dialogue. A report released by the US Senate's Permanent Subcommittee on Investigations cautions that CIs "attempt to export China's censorship of political debate and prevent discussion of potentially politically sensitive topics" (US Senate Permanent Subcommittee on Investigations 2019, p. 1). In Australia, Bob Katter, a member of the Australian House of Representatives, urged the prime minister to "declare the Confucius Institutes a political propaganda wing of the oppressive, dictatorial regime that is the Chinese Communist Party" (McIlroy 2020). These portrayals pose a significant challenge to CIs, as already alluded to in the introduction, and explored further in this section in more detail.

What They Do and How They Work

The operation of CIs has thus far featured significant flexibility and deliberate localization. This is evident in administrative, financial, and pedagogical domains. As for administrative management, CIs operate through a joint venture, simultaneously managed by Chinese and local administrators. How this comanagement works on the ground can vary. In Ethiopia, for instance, the CIs and CCs are largely managed by the Chinese side, with Ethiopian co-directors playing more of a symbolic role, whereas at some Russian and American CIs, the author observed local directors as shaping the agenda of the institutes.

As for financial operations, officially, when managed by Hanban, there were three funding models for Confucius Institutes: sponsorship by Hanban, sponsorship by the host university, or in many cases joint funds from Hanban and the host (Li & Tian 2015). The official CI Charter stipulated that for newly established CIs, the Chinese side should provide some start-up funds, and both sides contribute equally to annual project funds (Confucius Institute Headquarter/Hanban 2006). In the United States, we know that for every newly established CI, Hanban provided start-up capital ranging from $50,000 to $150,000, in addition to annual funds, CI teachers, and their salaries (US Government Accountability Office 2019). Host universities provided matching annual funds, as well as administrative support, teaching space, and housing support. The financial contributions of Hanban and host universities have varied across socioeconomic contexts. For instance, in many African countries, Hanban covered most of the costs, and local universities subsidized teachers' accommodation and teaching facilities (Li & Tian 2015).

It is not yet known whether and how the financial contributions from the Chinese side will change under the management of the new foundation, which appears to draw on funding from the twenty-seven participating entities, including major universities like the Beijing Language and Culture University (Chinese International Education Foundation 2020). At the 2020 Confucius Institutes Forum, Yang Wei, the chairman of the foundation, shared that the CIEF will raise funds for CIs, pay for training of CI leadership, and help develop marketing materials for individual CIs. Partner institutions are tasked with providing necessary facilitities for CIs and jointly raising funds for operations (Yang 2020). The specific proporitions of funding allocation have not been publicized. At the same time, the newly established Center for Language Education and Cooperation that replaced Hanban has committed to covering teacher training, including that of volunteers, as well as the design and management of teaching resources and selective Chinese scholarships and language camps (Center for Language Education and Cooperation).

When it comes to pedagogical operations, Hanban has produced some guidelines for teaching materials and curricula, but CI directors have been encouraged to adjust their teaching and cultural events in accordance with local customs and demands – a message articulated in several speeches of the last

Hanban director, Xu Lin (Xu & Li 2013). Training local teachers has also been a longstanding mission of Hanban and now also of the Chinese International Education Foundation.[4] Overall, localization, including varying degrees of comanagement, characterizes all facets of CI operations, from administration to finances and pedagogy. This feature is likely to become even more prominent with the shifts in the organizational structure of CIs.

The Role of CIs in China's Soft Power Efforts

The ambitious scale of CI expansion thus far appears to produce ambivalent effects on increasing China's soft power. The empirical evidence here is still scarce, and we mostly rely on indirect measures like the general state of bilateral relations, public opinion about China, or media coverage as a way of inferring the effects of CIs. As for bilateral relations, despite the concentrated presence of CIs in major countries, including the United States, Japan, and Australia, their relations with China have remained tense and arguably have even exacerbated over the years (Gil 2009). When it comes to measuring public sentiments, some studies, such as a survey of 1,300 students at two US high schools with Confucius Classrooms, show that students developed less favorable views of China over the course of an academic year (Green-Riley 2020). When taking media reports as a proxy for public opinion, there is a positive relationship between the proximity to an active CI and the tone of local media coverage about China globally (Brazys & Dukalskis 2019), though more research is needed on the role of intervening variables that have shaped this pattern.

Hanban itself, however, has interpreted success in more narrow terms by focusing on the scale of output. The few publicly accessible annual reports, such as that from 2009, for instance, assert that Hanban's efforts to promote Chinese-language teaching are successful despite the global financial crisis as more than 260,000 students had enrolled into CIs and CCs by the end of 2009 (International Society for Chinese Language Teaching Secretariat 2010). In this report, Hanban also draws on other quantitative measures, including the number of teachers sent overseas and the number of localized teaching materials produced over the course of the year. More recently, the 2019 report produced by Xiamen University, which operates as the Southern Base of Confucius Institutes Headquarters, illustrates success as registering 56,707 students at 15 CIs and 46 Confucius Classrooms, and holding 1,030 cultural events (Xiamen University). The 2019 International Chinese Language Education Conference

---

[4] The new foundation emphasized local teacher training as one of its core missions, see www .cief.org.cn/bthxjs. The original CI scholarship is also now titled as Chinese International Teacher Scholarship and managed by Hanban replacement, CLEC: https://cis.chinese.cn/account/login.

highlights that more than 25 million people worldwide are now learning Chinese (Liu 2019). How we evaluate soft power success is a theme that persists throughout this Element. In the case of CIs, it is clear that the evidence is scarce and inconclusive and that much depends on what is being measured. What is apparent, however, is that CIs still face significant challenges in shaping or shifting public perceptions about China. The two key challenges are political and operational.

Political Challenges

As for political or ideological frictions, public associations of CIs with China's political system hinder their cultural outreach. In the United States, American high school students are concerned with CIs as spreading propaganda and only presenting a partial picture of China in their teachings and immersive tours (Hubbert 2019). As already noted, many CIs have shut down due to political reasons. In Canada, jurisdictions such as Toronto, Manitoba, and New Brunswick have moved to opt out of partnerships with CIs because they present "a one-dimensional, uncritical look at China" (CBC News 2019). In Southeast Asia, Vietnam has been especially resistant to the establishment of CIs due to the grassroots perceptions of CIs as political organs, and the teaching of Chinese language as politically motivated to coopt or control Vietnamese people (Chinh 2014).

In Africa, the concerns are less explicit but still prescient. The university administrators in South Africa, for instance, actively debated the implications of hosting a CI on academic freedom, as well as on their relationships with other international partners, though these concerns have not sparked protests and withdrawals the way they have at some Western universities (Procopio 2015). At the University of Nairobi CI, local faculty expressed concerns with academic freedom, but more so with the broader power asymmetries associated with the lack of oversight over CIs in Kenya (Wheeler 2014).

The connection between political concerns and the lived experiences with censorship and self-censorship at CIs is debatable. On the one hand, self-censorship, especially when it comes to politically sensitive issues, such as Tibet and the Falun Gong, was uncovered at some CIs across regional contexts (Hartig 2015). As many students are already familiar with these topics through the media, self-censorship can become a credibility problem for CI teachers. Two students at University of Kentucky, for instance, told *Politico* that they recognize that CI teachers tend to gloss over negative aspects of China and promote "an overly rosy picture of Chinese culture" (Epstein 2018). One of the students emphasized that students can still take advantage of CI resources as long as they remain critical about the institute and learn more about China from other sources.

At the same time, some university administrators, including those directly involved with CIs in Britain, the United States, and Australia, present CIs as purely educational, cultural, and even practical initiatives, echoing the narratives of Hanban officials. "We have seen no evidence of the Chinese government using the university as a propaganda tool through CIs," noted a professor at Lampeter University in the United Kingdom (Yang 2010, p. 238).

Findings of the US Government Accountability Office attest to the validity of both perspectives – while some school officials and researchers express concerns over the screening process of CI teachers and the limits on discussions critical of China, others claim US schools hold decision-making power over hiring of CI teachers as well as all academic events on campus (US Government Accountability Office 2019).

While assessing the actual experiences with censorship at CIs would require more participant observations and extensive interviews, the suspicions toward CIs, at least in Western contexts, appear to be in large part driven by the preexisting conceptions or ideological beliefs about China. An in-depth study (Hubbert 2019) of CI classrooms in US high schools found that the trope of communism shaped the initial (and often the persisting) perceptions of CIs among American parents and students. In the United Kingdom, CI students also associated China with communism despite the efforts of teachers to introduce a more cultural and apolitical vision of China (Liu 2019). In fact, in some cases, the Chinese teachers' deliberate effort to depoliticize their teachings has backfired, as students interpreted them as repression or as further evidence of China's concealment of its dark past, such as the Tiananmen Massacre (Hubbert, 2019).

Media coverage of CIs, especially in the West, may further exacerbate or reinforce these preexisting ideological frames. The *New York Times*, for instance, portrays CIs as a soft power tool of the Chinese government but presents US influence as facilitating progress in other countries (Lueck et al. 2014). Likewise, *Politico* characterizes CIs as not only an effort to promote soft power but also as part of China's larger scheme to become a leading world power (Torres 2017). Outside of Western contexts, the picture is mixed. In Africa, for instance, in more vibrant democracies like Kenya, CIs have received some critical and investigative coverage. Eric Wamanji (2019), Kenyan foreign affairs analyst and journalist, cautions the expansion of CIs in Africa and the integration of Mandarin lessons into the school system as "a tool of propaganda in public diplomacy clandestinely embedded in narratives exalting the Chinese way of life and thought." In countries like Ethiopia where media strictly reports the official line on foreign affairs, especially on China, CI coverage is largely positive (Repnikova Forthcoming).

Overall, the association of CIs with China's political values, especially in the West, presents the primary challenge for the Chinese government. The Ministry of Education is clearly sensitive to the political associations of Confucius Institutes and their recent controversies in Western countries. The recent handing over of CI management to the newly established foundation is an attempt to disassociate CIs from the Chinese state. Zhang Yiwu, a professor at the Department of Chinese Language and Literature at Beijing University, argued that these changes will "help disperse misinterpretation of the network, which is merely for language teaching and cultural exchanges" (Zhang, quoted in Chen 2020). Yet it is uncertain whether this rebranding effort can shift existing ideological suspicions. David Stilwell, the assistant secretary of state for the Bureau of East Asian and Pacific Affairs, for instance, expressed distrust toward the new NGO: "So they become GONGOs, right – government-organized nongovernmental organizations. That's so communist" (US Department of State 2020). It doesn't help that these institutes are still named Confucius Institutes, and that the extent of indirect influence that the Ministry of Education will continue to exert over this initiative has not been clearly articulated.

Operational Challenges

Operational challenges or problematic implementation of CI projects on the ground is another important limitation of this initiative. The quantified evaluation metrics of CIs that focus on scale of activities come at the expense of qualitative metrics, such as teaching quality – a friction observed across regional/political contexts. In South Africa, for instance, while CIs have expanded their operations across the country, there is an underlying frustration among university administrators about the lack of advanced Mandarin students. "Students should progress. But they [the Chinese] don't get it. They want to have Chinese in more schools rather than deepening it down," noted a South African CI manager (Procopio 2015, pp. 117–8). In Germany, limited German skills of Chinese teachers inhibited them from interacting with students (Hartig 2012). At the University of Nairobi, the teaching agenda of CIs has fluctuated in accordance with "whatever the teacher wanted to do that day" (Wheeler 2014, p. 57), and students graduated only with basic conversational-level Chinese, not enough to use in employment. The teachers at the Nairobi CI also had little regional and cultural training about their destination (Wheeler 2014).

The quality of teaching materials is another area of concern. Chinese experts criticize teaching materials as lacking timeliness, as they tend to focus on history of China, present outdated depictions of China, and ignore local cultural contexts (Jin & Shi 2019; Zhan & Lu 2019). These concerns are also reflected in external evaluations of CI materials. James Hargett, a professor of East Asian studies at the University at Albany, for instance, notes that examples of activities used in CI textbooks are "geared toward life in China" unfamiliar to students in the United States (Hargett, cited in Peterson 2017). CI materials are also criticized as not fitting the pedagogical practices and standards of US universities. The US Government Accountability Office (2019) report on CIs found all the programs examined use Chinese-language books developed in the United States. The main reason is that "Chinese publishers have different ideas about how much time students can commit to language study" (US Government Accountability Office 2019, p. 15). The American CI director at Pace University also notes the inconsistent quality of textbooks received from China makes them only appropriate for beginner-level students (Peterson 2017).

Hanban officials have shown awareness of these quality issues. Xia Jianhui, the deputy director of Hanban, for instance, noted that many countries have reported the need for textbooks in their own languages (Bai 2014). In practice, Hanban has devoted great efforts to developing general language-teaching guidelines, enhancing teacher training capacity, recruiting and educating local Chinese language instructors, as well as localizing teaching materials and diversifying learning platforms (Li & Tucker 2013). These efforts do not appear to have yielded substantial results thus far.

Transforming teaching quality requires systemic changes, including implementation of institutional feedback mechanisms, as well adjustment of recruitment strategies to attract more qualified teachers. As for feedback channels, CI evaluations would have to shift from emphasizing growth toward focusing on quality. Measuring quality, however, is a cumbersome process that can also be politically sensitive, as it risks publicly revealing shortcomings of CI initiatives.

As for enticing high-caliber teachers and volunteers, recruitment standards would need to include some knowledge of foreign cultures or some past teaching experience, in addition to the basic requirements like 2-A Putonghua proficiency that have been used by Hanban. Recruiting better teachers also means creating stronger incentives for talented applicants. One of the main attractions of joining a CI project as a teacher or as a volunteer thus far appears to be a material one. In contrast to an average $716 salary of a recent college graduate in China (Mycos 2019 cited in Ye 2019), CI volunteers receive $800 or $1,000 monthly stipends, one-time $1,000 resettlement fee, and all living costs covered by Hanban (Office of Confucius Institute, Nanjing University). The salary gap between a job in China and at a CI, however, is starting to narrow, and many Chinese graduates with bachelor's or master's degrees in international Chinese-language teaching might worry about missing out on critical career opportunities in China if they go abroad (Xu & Bao 2019). New incentives, such as graduate school scholarships and post-return job promotions and placements, could help inspire more talented applicants.

Looking Ahead: Future Considerations about the CI Initiative

The current accounts of CIs tend to focus on their limitations and challenges, especially on political tensions surrounding this initiative. These political frictions are unlikely to soften, and CIs will continue to face pushback in Western countries, including more shutdowns and investigations. It remains to be seen whether the Chinese International Education Foundation will manage to transform Western perceptions of CIs. Other than general statements by the new chairman, little information is publicly available about the workings of this NGO. Beyond the name change, we haven't seen any substantive transformations on the ground yet, and no reevaluations of the CI project by Western politicians as a result of this institutional shift.

Despite the setbacks in Western contexts, however, CIs can still yield domestic benefits for the Chinese party-state, as well as soft power gains in non-Western contexts. Domestically, the CI initiative carries cultural and economic advantages. As for the former, Chinese-language popularity internationally can bolster domestic pride in Chinese culture. Chinese domestic media tries to foster this sentiment. A recent Xinhua report, for instance, said that CIs struggle to meet the increasing global demands for Chinese-language learning due to "China's rising international influence" (Xia et al. 2020). The Chinese Bridge Proficiency Competition – an international competition organized by Hanban – has turned into a widely broadcasted annual event watched by millions of Chinese citizens. On the economic front, CIs can also boost China's higher-education internationalization by allowing Chinese universities to build up their brands and attract more foreign students and revenues. More analyses exploring domestic as well as economic and cultural linkages would help expand our understanding of CIs beyond the strictly external political lens.

As for CIs potential in non-Western contexts, Chinese-language teaching continues to be in high demand in the Global South. In my research, I found that Hanban has considered Africa to be the most dynamic region, and that the demand for CIs on the continent appears to outpace that of supply at this point. Since 2012, the number of students enrolled at CIs in Africa has increased by almost 36 percent every year (Zhao 2018). Similar trends are found in Central

Asia and Latin America (He 2019; Shayakhmetova 2018). In Kyrgyzstan, as of 2013, a country with a population of 5.4 million, as many as 150,000 people were learning the Chinese language (Fan & Zou 2013). In Latin America, as of 2018, Hanban has established forty CIs in twenty-one countries (Wang & Dang 2018). While much of this attraction to CIs might be rooted in practical motivations, in contrast to developed countries like the United States, where students appear to distinguish between the benefits of Chinese language and their (absent) "desire" for China (Hubbert 2019), in contexts where China has a more omnipresent economic and political influence, the pragmatic gravitation may fuse with admiration and even enchantment with Chinese culture. These potential linkages between pragmatic and cultural attraction are worth exploring in future studies.

3 China's Quest for Global Media Power

Introduction

This section engages with China's evolving global communication influence through state media channels or what's officially referred to in Chinese writings as external propaganda or publicity (*duiwai xuanchuan* 对外宣传) and more recently as international communication (*guoji chuanbo* 国际传播). China's external propaganda has a long history, dating to the Mao era, when Mao himself promoted party policies and ideologies through print media and set up the party agencies for external communication, such as the International Press Bureau (国际新闻局) under the General Information Administration (新闻总署). From 1978 onward, China's external communication has experienced significant evolution and expansion.

During the Reform and Opening Up period, from 1978 to 1999, external propaganda was revitalized through the launch of new institutions, as well as through global expansion of Chinese state media. As for institutionalization, the by now well-known State Council Information Office was founded in 1991. It works under the guidance of the CCP's Central Propaganda Department that oversees all media control and propaganda initiatives, including domestic and external messaging. In this phase, Chinese state media also witnessed their first global expansion since the Cultural Revolution. In contrast to the Mao era when Xinhua News Agency mostly assigned reporters to selective countries with overlapping ideological interests, starting in 1978, Chinese state media began expanding international bureaus globally. Xinhua, for instance, had 101 international bureaux by the end of the twentieth century (Jiang & Zhang 2019).

After China's accession to the World Trade Organization (WTO) in 2001, Chinese leaders became even more concerned with the status and influence of their global media. In 2009, the "going-out" media policy was officially launched with the focus on Chinese media broadcasting "China's voice," and Chinese global media companies competing with Western media conglomerates. The central government committed $6 billion to this effort, designating key state media as "pioneers of this undertaking" (Hu & Ji 2012, p. 33). Xinhua received one-third of the budget (Hu & Ji 2012, p. 33) and used it to launch CNC World News, its English television network, and to expand its international bureaus. CCTV, China's Central Television channel, has expanded its broadcasting into multiple languages, including Arabic, Spanish, French, and Russian. In 2009, the *Global Times*, published under the *People's Daily*, launched its English-language edition, and *China Daily*, the first national English-language newspaper, launched the US edition (Hu & Ji 2012, p. 34). A special focus of the Chinese media going-out push has been in Africa that some see as a testing ground of its larger global initiatives (Lim & Bergin 2018). In 2012, CGTN, the international arm of CCTV, opened its Africa headquarters in Nairobi in 2012, and *China Daily* launched its Africa edition.

Since 2013, global communication has been further reprioritized in line with Xi Jinping's Belt and Road Initiative (BRI) and his emphasis on soft power and discourse power (*huayu quan* 话语权). Several key shifts have taken place. First, we see centralization of external propaganda management. In 2018, the key Chinese state global media conglomerates, CCTV, China Radio International, and China National Radio have been merged into the Voice of China under the direct supervision of the Central Publicity Department (the renamed Propaganda Department). The strategy of spreading Chinese voice via partnerships with local media has also become more prominent in recent years – something explained further in this section. We also see Chinese state media expanding into more locations, especially in Africa and Latin America.

This section explores China's international communication in detail, with a focus on external broadcasting, as it has received more attention than China's international print and radio. The analysis demonstrates that similarly to CIs, the grand ambition of the Chinese party-state in expanding its media presence is at odds with the implementation of this initiative. The section proceeds with discussing the key motivations for China's global media expansion, the approaches deployed, and the effects observed thus far.

Motivations for Expanding Global Media Reach

There are political, market, and societal rationales behind China's global media expansion in the reform era and in particular in the past eight years under Xi Jinping. The core driving motivation has long been that of improving China's image – a concern that has become most pronounced under Xi who directed journalists to "tell the China story well" (Xinhua News Agency 2017). This storytelling is aimed at both explaining China to the world and correcting Western misconceptions about China.

As for explaining China, the constructive storytelling agenda is distinct from that of other authoritarian powers like Russia, more interested in manufacturing a negative image of its main rival, the United States, than in telling its own story (Rawnsley 2015). At the same time, China's ambition in global communication is at least in part defensive, centered on competing for discourse power or "equality of discourse with the West, and in particular for the means to convey its viewpoints as its global influence and responsibilities grew" (Marsh 2018, p. 144). The West is often portrayed in Chinese official rhetoric as misconstructing the global narrative about China (Sun 2015), and Chinese media as reasserting China's voice on the global stage.

Beyond correcting Western stereotypes, for now only a minority of voices in China advocate for a more aggressive global media agenda (Sun 2015), but there are signs that this might be changing. In recent years, we have seen the emergence of the so-called Wolf Warrior Diplomacy, whereby Chinese officials publicize harsh defensive and at times offensive rhetoric on Twitter. Many Chinese academic writings focus on *Russia Today* (RT) as an inspiration or as a successful example in external propaganda (Cheng 2013). A scholar from Jiangsu Normal University, for instance, commends RT as "successfully fighting back against slanders from Western media, breaking the West-led news communication system, and effectively improving Russia's national image" (Yan 2020). How these constructive, defensive, and offensive agendas continue to coexist in China's global communication is something to watch closely in the years to come.

There are also economic or market motivations behind China's global media drive. China's state media have evolved into "market-oriented conglomerates" that are motivated to expand their audiences in the same way as major Western media outlets (Zhao 2013). Chinese media leaders emphasize users or audiences. "Wherever our millions and millions of users lead us, CGTN will follow," noted Jiang Heping, the director of CGTN (CGTN 2017). A shift in some state media content from more ideological toward more market-oriented coverage also signals an evolving concern with readership (Madrid-Morales 2016). Other than engagement with audiences, global expansion is motivated by competition for resources from the government allocated under the media going-out policy (Guo & Lye 2011).

The interests of Chinese media practitioners and the broader public also align when it comes to media expansion. Cosmopolitan sensibilities of Chinese media editors and managers working for state news outlets favorably position them toward shaping global narratives. Rather than being pressured by the state to carry out global initiatives, these managers "have long had a desire to have a genuine dialogue with the West" (Zhao 2013, p. 23). The growing nationalist sentiments across the Chinese public also push for a more extensive engagement of Chinese media in discourse competition (Zhao 2013). In fact, China's online nationalism has become its own distinctive phenomenon, as Chinese netizens now partake in global public opinion battles voluntarily via Western social media platforms, like Twitter and Facebook (Repnikova & Fang 2018). When it comes to state media expansion, therefore, there is an apparent convergence in political, market, as well as bottom-up voices, including those of journalists and netizens in igniting China's quest to play a more powerful role in the global communication system (Zhao 2013).

China's External Broadcasting Operations: Between Innovation and Constraints

Chinese Media as a Dynamic Force

The deliberately constructive tone and increasingly localized content production and distribution present distinctive innovative features of China's global communication approach. Constructive journalistic practice – something rooted in China's domestic journalism tradition (Repnikova 2017) – is understood as a contra-narrative to the West, especially in the context of China in Africa. Chinese scholars present constructive reporting as neither positive nor uncritical, but as "an approach that combines the techniques of critical journalism with narratives that explore solutions" (Zhang & Matingwina 2016, p. 24). It is meant to empower the readers. At some international forums, Chinese scholars directly advocate for this approach as an alternative to Western media's focus on crises and failures – an approach that has attracted some interest in developing contexts like Africa (Zhang 2014), at least among the elites with close business interests with China (Wan 2015). At the same time, Chinese global reporting also increasingly features elements of Western journalistic professionalism, especially in coverage of events that are not immediately sensitive for Chinese leadership, such as the Iraq War, for which the CCTV International coverage won praise from Western media competitors (Liang 2012).

Localization (*bentuhua* 本土化) of media production and distribution is another important feature of China's global media. Localization of production teams involves hiring local media professionals, particularly for reporting roles, whereas the editorial and managerial control still remains with Beijing (Brady 2015). These hiring patterns are especially notable in Chinese state media bureaus in Washington DC, and Nairobi, where local correspondents make up a large proportion of staff. In-depth studies of Chinese media headquarters in Africa, such as that of CCTV Africa, find that this form of localization is not purely symbolic, but that local journalists are given significant resources and opportunities to cover issues that other (Western) media might not (Gagliardone 2013).

Chinese outlets also localize distribution of content, including via business partnerships with local media outlets that involve content-sharing agreements, as well as through China's acquisitions of local outlets. As for content sharing, *China Daily* has struck deals with at least thirty foreign newspapers, including *The New York Times*, *The Wall Street Journal*, and *The Washington Post*, to carry its paid insert, the *China Watch* (Lim & Bergin 2018). Freedom House points out that in digital format, *China Watch* appears as an online feature, blending in with the main content produced by these media outlets (Cook 2020).

A recent analysis of China–Latin America media partnerships (Geall & Soutar 2018) shows that content distribution agreements are often incorporated into larger frameworks of media cooperation. Following the signing of high-level media partnership agreements, for instance, *China Daily* placed a paid *China Watch* supplement in various Argentinian newspapers. In recent years, there has also been some pushback against collaborating with *China Daily*, as some media outlets have cancelled the supplement, including the *Sydney Morning Herald* (Meade 2020) and the *Daily Telegraph* (Waterson and Jones 2020).

Content distribution agreements can also work through diaspora connections (Sun 2010b), as transnational Chinese elites are eager to monetize on China's quest for media expansion (Sun 2010b). In 2007, Tommy Jiang, a Melbourne-based migrant and media mogul, secured a deal with China Radio International (CRI), which he considers "the ultimate hallmark of his success" (Sun 2010b, p. 128). Based on the agreement, Jiang's Perth Chinese Radio 104.9 FM now broadcasts ten hours of CRI programs every day in both English and Chinese. On a larger scale, *Financial Times* finds that "party-affiliated outlets have been reprinting or broadcasting their content in at least 200 nominally independent Chinese-language publications around the world" (Feng 2018).

Under Xi, international business agreements have evolved into more direct acquisitions or takeovers of Western media outlets, referred to by Chinese policymakers as "buying the boat" (*jiechuan chuhai*借船出海). A Reuters investigation identifies at least thirty-three radio stations in fourteen countries that have CRI as the majority shareholder (Qing & Shiffman 2015). It is also important to note that the United Front Work Department, a central organ of the

CCP Central Committee, oversees financial transfers to foreign media, including buying advertising and acquiring shares.

Chinese Media Expansion as a Fractured Enterprise

Alongside these rhetorical and operational innovations, there are also inherent contradictions in China's going-out media campaign, including the challenge of conveying a credible and distinctive voice, as well as the fractured localization practices of Chinese media. As for credibility, Chinese state media face a similar challenge to that of Confucius Institutes in terms of their affiliation with the Chinese Communist Party. For media outlets, this affiliation is more pronounced in multilayered political control that results in precensored content. In addition to the oversight from major party and state bureaucracies like the Central Propaganda Department and the State Council Information Office, the key state media outlets engaged in external propaganda are internally governed by senior staff directly appointed by the Central Propaganda Department (Brady 2009a). The media gatekeepers are summoned to the Central Propaganda Department for briefings (*tongqihui* 通气会) to receive evaluations and instructions, including guidance on sensitive topics (Zhao 2008). The actual content management, including censorship, varies across different media. Xinhua News Agency is known for being more risk averse, as the official mouthpiece of the party, whereas the CGTN has deliberately positioned itself as more market oriented.

Given the domestic considerations of presenting unity and upholding stability, Chinese media can occasionally capitalize on their resources in creatively reporting on major natural disasters like the Sichuan earthquake or external crises like the Iraq War, but they are less capable of objective and transparent reporting of routine political and societal events in China (Sun 2010a). This means that the coverage of China to global audiences is always somewhat partial and skewed toward the positive angle.

Related to this, the constructive genre that defines much of Chinese reporting compromises its credibility. In the case of CGTN operations in Nairobi, for instance, African colleagues often reinterpret constructive reporting as positive reporting – at once embracing the opportunity to tell more positive stories about Africa but also questioning the credibility of overwhelmingly positive framing (Marsh 2017). CCTV's Ebola outbreak coverage confirmed some of these concerns. Whereas the constructive framing channeled voices of African elites, it overlooked the more tragic angles, including stories of victims themselves (Marsh 2017). Frictions between credible journalism and propaganda are also present in Chinese media reporting of domestic news for international audiences. A comparative analysis of the coverage of the 2015 Tianjin explosion by CGTN and CNN found that while the two networks prioritized neutrality and had similar framing strategies, CGTN's coverage was more hesitant to attribute responsibility to government officials (Fearon & Rodrigues 2019).

The credibility of Chinese media is also hampered by its frequent focus on critiquing the West at the expense of explaining China's own positions. CGTN's *Africa Live* show, for instance, widely critiques the actions and policies of the West in Africa and yet does not articulate a distinctive vision of what China stands for, beyond its apparent dissatisfaction with the West (Zhang 2013). During the Trump administration, *China Daily* actively criticized Trump and the US political system but only indirectly hinted at the attractiveness of China (Pan et al. 2020).

There are also apparent tensions in localization efforts of Chinese media production practices. Despite hiring a large number of local staff in Africa, Chinese media outlets have thus far not succeeded in creating a shared corporate identity that would bring together Chinese and African journalists (Gagliardone & Pál 2017). The experiences of African journalists working for Chinese state media organizations further reveal notable hierarchies of Chinese over Africans hidden beneath the narratives of equality and mutuality (Umejei 2018). These hierarchies are not unique to Africa. Interviews with foreign staff at CGTN in Beijing found that they are often given marginal roles and are constrained from creating content or making organizational decisions (Varrall 2020). A foreign journalist working at CGTN states that "they're willing to pay Westerners, but they are not willing to listen to them" (Varrall 2020). Content localization, especially in unfamiliar and highly competitive contexts, like the United States, has also been a struggle. While Chinese media are encouraged to localize from the top, limited awareness of local audiences and loose connections between the headquarters and the local team make for uncertain outcomes (Zou 2018).

Global Reception to Chinese Media: Ambivalent Results

The challenges discussed here are reflected in a mixed reception toward Chinese media content. For now, we know most about the reception in the Global South. Despite Chinese media's recent expansion there, especially in Africa, the attraction to these outlets on the ground is still limited. In Latin America, for instance, China's Spanish-language Central Television Station, CCTV-E, faces a dual problem of low recognition (and visibility) and low credibility (Morales 2018; Ye & Albornoz 2018). Claudia Trevisan, the executive director of the Brazil-China Business Council and a former journalist, asserts the following:

> Most of them [Latin American news outlets] use American, European news agencies to get news from China. ... CGTN does not have service in Portuguese, so it's irrelevant in Brazil, which is one third of the population of Latin America. They do have a service in Spanish, but it's very unattractive, very boring, stiff. And all the indications are that their ratings are very very low. (Trevisan, cited in Economy 2021)

The more informal style of *Russia Today* appears to be more credible to Latin American audiences than the more official style of CCTV (Morales 2018).

In Africa, interviews and surveys of selective African audiences uncover similar trends. In South Africa, for instance, a survey of more than 100 journalists from diverse media outlets found that they rarely access Chinese media sources, seeing them as unappealing and less credible than those of Western news outlets (Wasserman 2012). In Kenya, members of the university and media community see China's economic prowess rather than media outreach behind its soft power in Kenya. The interviewees were largely unaware of CCTV, and those who were held little trust in it (Maweu 2016). A research survey of about 200 mostly young private sector employees in Nairobi found that the most watched foreign media channel is CNN (Zhang & Mwangi 2016).

In major industrialized countries, the appeal of Chinese media is also limited. In the United States, Freedom House estimates that there are more people watching online videos of NTDTV, a channel founded by the Falun Gong, than CGTN, which rarely generates more than a few hundred views on YouTube (*The Economist* 2018). In Europe, an audit in 2014 found that 94 percent of copies of *China Daily*'s weekly European edition were given away rather than sold at the marked price of $2.65 per copy (*The Economist* 2018). Across Asia, following domestic media outlets, the US media rather than Chinese outlets remain the dominant source of news (Bley 2019).

Looking Ahead: The Future of Chinese Global Media

In contrast to the dwindling international presence of major Western media outlets, China's state media have undergone a significant global expansion over the past two decades. Whereas the CI initiative positions itself as more cultural and educational, Chinese official statements about global communication carry a more explicit political tone, with media being directly tied to the project of soft power, discourse competition, and more broadly China's rise in the international system.

Despite the innovative practices of China's international media outlets, especially when it comes to localization, the dual challenge of credibility and brand recognition is likely to persist. The credibility concerns discussed earlier have now morphed into associations of Chinese state media with sharp power in Western policy narratives. In 2020, Chinese state media have been labeled as foreign agents in the United States; in 2021, CGTN's broadcasting license was revoked in the United Kingdom. Concerns have also emerged about China's local media partnerships directly infringing on freedom of expression. In 2018, for instance, South Africa's second-largest media group, Independent Media, fired a journalist after he published a critical column about China's activities in Xinjiang. This caused alarms, as Chinese investors hold a 20 percent stake in this media outlet (RSF 2018). New controversies have also erupted about co-optation of Mandarin language diasporic outlets via investments and invitations for trainings in China (Cook 2020).

Other than carving out some distance from the Chinese party-state, Chinese state media will continue to face tough competition for brand recognition with major Western outlets and also with other emerging non-Western global players, like *Russia Today*. The content featured on Chinese state outlets is not as provocative as that of RT, but also not as objective and professional as that produced by Western news outlets. As Chinese media itself has gone through significant Westernization, there is also the difficulty of carving out a unique voice beyond that of constructive journalism.

The dual challenge of credibility and recognition is significant, and yet it is premature to dismiss China's global media push as a failure. First, we shouldn't underestimate the adaptive capacity of Chinese media. While heavily controlled, state media outlets are increasingly encouraged to engage with audiences and to improvise in accordance with local contexts, including by extensively relying on local journalists for their reporting. Over time, local journalists at Chinese outlets, including freelancers, might be able to reshape Chinese media practices. There is already some evidence of that in the African context, where African journalists have influenced Chinese managers on the ground to produce more balanced and professional coverage (Gagliardone 2013). More analyses of Chinese media operations in diverse global contexts would help map out these adaptations and interactions.

Second, whereas Chinese media content may not appeal to wider global publics, Chinese media and communication infrastructure arguably present a more powerful, yet controversial soft power channel for China. China's involvement in global communication infrastructure is especially pronounced on the African continent. StarTimes is now the biggest digital TV provider with 10 million subscribers across the continent, Shenzhen-based Transsion Holdings is one of Africa's top smartphone makers (Mohanmmed 2015), and Huawei and ZTE have taken over the telecom infrastructure in several African countries (Workneh 2016). In recent years, the reach of China's communication infrastructure has also expanded to other regions. Since Huawei's 2009 contract to build a 4G network in Norway, the company has expanded operations to more than 170 countries worldwide (Feng 2019). As of 2019, as many as fifty-four countries, including Italy, Germany, Spain, and South Korea, have allowed Huawei to set up 5G networks. Only four countries, Australia, Japan, New Zealand, and the United States have banned such activities (Feng 2019). China's communication infrastructure ambitions are now also part of the Belt and Road Initiative, coined as the Digital Silk Road – the policy aimed at supporting Chinese exporters who work in everything from telecommunications to e-commerce and smart city technology. China has signed Digital Silk Road agreements with sixteen countries and has spent an estimated $79 billion DSR projects. This is likely only the beginning to China's much larger foray into the communication technology market, especially in the Global South (Kurlantzick 2020).

How and whether China's communication infrastructure plays into its global image is still uncertain, but there are signs that infrastructure provision is connected with ideational power. StarTimes, for instance, fuses an ideological dimension into its digital TV platforms in Africa, as the company incorporates a lot of Chinese content into its subscription plans (Madrid-Morales 2018). StarTimes's Sino Drama channel broadcasts and dubs popular Chinese TV dramas into local languages. As of 2019, twenty-one African voice actors and actresses are working at the Star Times Beijing-based dubbing center; they have dubbed more than 20,000 Chinese drama episodes for African viewers (CGTN 2019).

The popularity of Chinese phone brands in Africa may end up facilitating a more positive image of China among African youth. Trassion's three phone brands, Tecno, Itel, and Infinix, are designed primarily for African consumers and priced between $15 and $200 (Marsh 2018). China's involvement in the telecom sector in Africa may enhance the official desire of working with China in other domains. The ZTE and Huawei's partnership with Ethiopian Telecom, for instance, has crystallized the appeal of China's policy of noninterference for the Ethiopian government (Workneh 2016).

At the same time, China's expansion into the global communication infrastructure can also carry adverse effects for its soft power. In many Western countries, security concerns about China's involvement in the 5G infrastructure are growing. As of June 2021, at least fifteen countries, including Australia (BBC 2018), Sweden (Keane 2021), Canada (Ljunggren 2020) and Japan (Tao 2018), among other industrialized economies, have either blocked Huawei or implemented more restrictive policies. In the Global South, China's technology, while accessible, is also often associated with low quality and therefore deemed as less desirable. Yet, the potential for Chinese soft power to be channeled through the "hardware" of communication technology is arguably still more significant than via the "software" of its media content. The dependency on Chinese technology will only continue to grow, especially in developing countries, and what China offers is more cost effective in comparison with Western competitors. It is timely to investigate further the relationship between Chinese communication infrastructure companies and the party-state, as well as how the infrastructure provision plays into the larger image of China across global contexts.

4 China as the Education Hub

This section delves into educational exchanges, which encompass a variety of activities, including short-term trainings, scientific exchanges, and Chinese-language and other professional/academic degree programs for international students. After about two decades of internationalizing China's education system by learning from Japan and from the West, starting in early 2000s, the official objective has shifted toward establishing China as a major center of knowledge production and as an attractive international destination for education and training. From 1978 to 2018, the number of international students in China increased from 1,236 (Wen 2013) to 492,200 (Shi & Hu 2019). As of 2018, most international students came from Korea, Thailand, Pakistan, India, and the United States (Zhao 2019), but the fastest-growing intake is from African countries, with the numbers rising by nearly forty times over fifteen years (from 2,186 in 2003 to 81,562 in 2018; see Zhao 2019). Based on statistics published by the Ministry of Education, from 2000 to 2016, the Chinese language remains the most popular subject, and the number of students majoring in Western medicine, engineering, and management is rising quickly.

The Chinese government has also sponsored a variety of short-term trainings that take visitors (primarily officials and journalists) from other countries for tours of China that combine cultural immersion with knowledge exchange. These trainings have been especially prominent in Africa, where thousands of officials have now been trained in China, raising alarms in the West about China's growing ideological influence on the continent. Some of these trainings have also evolved into institutionalized fellowships, such as the ten-month media and cultural exchange fellowship launched in 2014 at the China Africa Press Center – a program that has recently expanded to hosting journalists from Asia-Pacific countries.

This section proceeds to explain the motivations behind China's education internationalization push, as well as the mixed reception toward China's educational offerings. It demonstrates the relatively strong potential of education as a soft power mechanism for China in contrast to other instruments, along with its underlying frictions rooted in the merging of hard and soft power motivations, and the unresolved racial tensions that tint the China experience, especially for visitors from African nations.

Motivations

The combination of political and economic motivations in internationalizing higher education and professional trainings most clearly demonstrates China's integration of soft and hard power. As for political rationale, Chinese authorities frame educational exchange as an important part of its "people-to-people" diplomacy and soft power. In 2016, the CPC Central Committee and the State Council issued the "Opinion on the Work of the Opening-Up of Education in the New Era" – the first guiding document (纲领性文件) that directs China's education opening-up since the founding of the PRC. In addition to broadly linking education exchange to China's soft power and the China Dream, this document encourages "gathering patriotic power of the vast population who study overseas, taking the initiative to promote China's developments and accomplishments, actively bringing into play the promotional abilities of foreign students and teachers in China, and actively communicating Chinese ideas" (The CPC Central Committee and the State Council 2016). In 2017, the Ministry of Education (2017) emphasized cultivating foreign students' identification with and integration into China through cultural events to foster understanding and friendly perceptions of China. Some experts consider the lived experience in China as part of an educational exchange to have a more direct or linear impact on soft power. By studying in China, foreign students will "be sensitized to Chinese viewpoints and interests with knowledge of the Chinese language, society, culture, history, and politics" (Yang 2007, p. 25) and eventually end up shaping the China policy of their home countries once they return and become local opinion leaders (Yang and Xie 2015, cited in Metzgar 2016).

These political associations with education exchanges in China go back to the Mao era, predating the emergence of the concept of soft power. Historians of that period note that "one of the main fronts of the cultural-ideological Cold War was occupied by young people" (Graziani et al. 2017, p. 195). Similarly to today, investments into young foreign students were shaped by hopes of them turning into important friends and allies of China. Under Mao, however, there was a more pronounced ideological motivation, with Mao himself teaching guerrilla warfare and propagating global anti-colonial struggle to foreign guests (Lovell 2019). Students were also carefully preselected as sympathetic to

Figure 2 Nyerere visit to China in 1968 (Photo by Keystone-France\Gamma-Rapho via Getty Image)

China's ideology and holding powerful political positions in their home countries (Lovell 2019). One of the famous African guests invited to China in 1959, for instance, was the secretary general of the Zanzibar Nationalist Party, Abdulrahman Mohammed Babu, who later went on to serve for several years as the East and Central Africa correspondent for the Xinhua News Agency, promoting Mao's vision of armed struggle and revolution (Lovell 2019). Another frequent visitor to China was Julius Nyerere – anti-colonial leader and the first president of independent Tanzania whose governance style was deeply inspired by Mao's teachings and practices, especially by the idea of "self-reliance" manifested in China's Great Leap Forward (Lovell 2019).

Given the openness of China to the world, and the scale of China's higher educational internationalization and foreign exchanges in the reform era, the selection approach for foreign dignitaries and students has become less targeted, but there is still a prioritization of certain regions as indicative of strategic geopolitical goals. The Chinese government's increasing scholarships to students from BRI countries (more than 250,000 students in 2018), for instance, presents a "channel to building foreign students' awareness and acceptance of China's foreign policy" (Jain 2020, p. 542). The recent government scholarship schemes also align with national strategic needs. In 2012, for instance, reflecting China's diplomatic priorities, thirteen bilateral special scholarship programs were established, including China-Mongolia, China-Tanzania, and China-Egypt initiatives, as well as new educational exchange initiatives launched with major powers, such as the United States, European Union, and Russia.

In addition to a political rationale that has historic legacies in the Mao era, there are also apparent economic motivations behind the internationalization of higher education in the reform era. China's neoliberal education restructuring is conducive to recruitment of international students (Haugen 2013). As with other previously state-owned sectors, such as media and health care, the Chinese government has cut education subsidies, delegating financing responsibilities to universities themselves. As of 2020, out of seventy-five Chinese universities that are under direct management of the Ministry of Education, more than sixty have reported a decrease in revenues from the state, amounting to more than $1.84 billion (*Southern Metropolis Daily* 2020). This means that revenues from international students present an attractive opportunity. In contrast to the Mao era when most foreign students came on government-funded scholarships, the majority of international students in China today are self-funded, including those coming from the Global South (Haugen 2013).

Other than direct monetary gains from international students, there are also indirect commercial benefits for recruiting certain types of foreign professionals. In Nepal, for instance, Chinese scholarship schemes target individuals with existing government networks and scientific expertise that can help support China's economic interests in the country (Jain 2020). China's recruitment of foreign experts also aligns with its development of strategic sectors domestically. For instance, the state-driven Made in China 2025 campaign – a plan initiated in 2015 that aims to upgrade its manufacturing industry to become more technology focused – encourages "introducing advanced technologies and high-end talents" (State Council 2015). The High-End Foreign Expert Recruitment Program, previously and better known as the Thousand Talents, supports the development of four key areas: strategic technology and development, industrial skill innovation, social and ecological construction, and agricultural and rural revitalization (Ministry of Science and Technology 2020). The political motives, therefore, are bolstered and reinforced by commercial and economic ones, which makes for a fast expansion of China's internationalization of higher education and training. Yet, it also creates unique challenges, as explained further in this section.

Implementation: The Divergent Experiences with China as an Education Destination

The story of China's education exchanges as a soft power channel is a complicated one. On the one hand, some visitors' positive impressions about China suggest that education exchanges strengthen China's soft power. On the other hand, the underlying issue of mixed quality of the China experience, including pedagogical concerns and racial frictions, diminishes the potential soft power gains from China's educational offerings.

As for positive impressions, a survey of 270 recipients of Chinese Government Scholarships studying in Shanghai and Beijing found that 91.6 percent of respondents "were positive about the likely impact of the scholarship program in promoting the long-term friendship between China and their home country" (Dong & Chapman, 2008, p. 165). Most of the survey respondents were happy about their choice of coming to China, and about 77 percent were satisfied with the overall experience. Those especially committed to the program tended to also derive most satisfaction from it. Other than satisfaction with the overall experience, some participants also leave China with a deeper sense of understanding and appreciation of some facets of Chinese culture, such as the Chinese work ethic. Some Kenyan students educated in China contrasted the strong work ethic of Chinese students and educators with less committed public attitudes toward work in their own country (King 2013). One returnee from China describes Kenya's work culture in disparaging terms: "The people here are 'idle'; they don't come in and work. And they lack the discipline. What could be brought in from China is good governance of the institutions, also of student behavior. The students monitor each other and look after each other" (King 2013, p. 79). Other than admiring Chinese culture, some African students also serve as cultural representatives or ambassadors, as they introduce Chinese culture to their countries, as well as promote African culture in China (Li 2018). For instance, in the summer of 2009, African residents in Beijing founded the Young African Professionals and Students organization (YAPS) – an inclusive group of Africans from different countries and professions. Lefifi Tebogo, YAPS chairwoman and a business consultant based in Beijing explained: "We are culture, education and industry ambassadors and promoters. For China-Africa, we hope to promote Africa as a brand of choice. We will create more opportunities and a solid support base while YAPS members are studying or developing their careers in the China-Africa realm" (Tegogo, cited in *Global Times* 2010).

Other than cultural appreciation, some students, and especially official trainees from countries in the Global South, admire and even adopt China's worldview and foreign policy vision as a result of their immersive experience in China. Some African journalists who come for trainings express skeptical views about Western media coverage of China-Africa relations and come away with an appreciation of China's generosity and a view of "China-Africa relations as a partnership based on respect and among equals" (Benabdallah 2020, p. 105). Their positive impressions primarily emerge from their experiences with China's hospitality and the relationships formed with Chinese interlocutors (Benabdallah 2020). The impressive hospitality, including banquets and all paid for extravagant tours of China, impacts journalist participants on professional and personal levels, making them more likely to convey a positive narrative of China-Africa relations to their domestic audiences. The pro-China narratives and sentiments are also formed via relationship building with Chinese hosts that foster mutual trust (Benabdallah 2020). Networking also carries a pan-African dimension. African students from across the continent network with one another on Chinese campuses, with the help of Chinese professors and African studies centers. African students appear to acquire a renewed connection with their own continent through the lens of China, with Chinese faculty positioning themselves as empowering pan-African solidarity (Li 2018).

At the same time, the mixed quality of China's education exchanges diminishes China's soft power gains. The concerns with quality are raised by both the recipients and the hosts. As for recipients, one extensive survey of African students' experiences in China revealed largely negative feedback about the programs, with fewer than half of respondents rating their experience as "good" or "excellent" (Gillespie 2001). Some doctoral students found the attitudes of their Chinese hosts to be careless and shared that they felt neglected during their stay. Other students were particularly disappointed with program and course design, the level of mutuality, and access to technology and industrial sites (Gillespie 2001). Another group of students was generally content with Chinese-language teaching but criticized the pedagogical approach that in their view discouraged critical thinking (Haugen 2013). One African student compared the academic environment in China with that in Africa and in the West: "To study in China is better than in most African countries. But the problem here is [that the] Chinese are not supposed to criticize the lecturer. . . . Not like in African countries and Europe and America where you can criticize, give another idea. . . . Here, you have to accept and full stop. Then you close your mind, you don't open your mind" (Haugen 2013, p. 327). Some participants in short-term training programs also cynically reflected on the content introduced in the teachings. Alpha Daffae Senkpeni, a reporter and editor at Liberia's *FrontPage Africa*, traveled to China through the China-Africa Press

Center in 2017. Reflecting on his visit, he states, "this trip was designed to sell China's image, yes, but I am not going to trade my principles for some Chinese belief about journalism" (Senkpeni, cited in McCormick 2019). These concerns with quality have especially escalated during the pandemic. Many international students have complained about not being able to return to China and struggling with their studies online. An online group called the China Students has regularly appealed to the Ministry of Education and to the Foreign Affairs Ministry to resolve the problem but has not received a satisfying response so far. The *South China Morning Post* reports that as of 2021 about half a million international students still await their return to China. "It's not just the lack of human-to-human interaction which is a problem, but it's also the students are so frustrated, and they feel like they're actually being treated badly and being neglected," shared Mulvey, an expert on foreign students in China, quoted in SCMP (Lau 2021). The treatment of international students during the pandemic is likely to haunt Chinese efforts at internationalizing education for years to come.

Other than academic, administrative, and ideological concerns, there is also the persisting issue of racial discrimination. Stories of institutional racial discrimination come up in interviews with African students who share that they are treated differently from white students by university administrators (Haugen 2013, p. 328). A student from South Africa who was getting her degree at Zhejiang Normal University referred to what she found to be a common sentiment of "invisibility" among African students on Chinese university campuses (Pagano 2018). In contrast to white students who are efficiently and enthusiastically served by the university bureaucracy, African students are often made to feel as if they do not exist by being deliberately sidelined (Pagano 2018). These contemporary racialized encounters are predated by more explicit racial clashes between Chinese and African students on Chinese university campuses. In 1988–9, for instance, dormitories of African students in major Chinese cities were attacked and destroyed by thousands of Chinese students fueled by racist rumors (Dikötter 1992).

While Chinese officials and university administrators have consistently denied the presence of institutional racism at Chinese universities, Chinese writings do express concerns about the quality of the educational experience for international students. Chinese experts lament the low admission standards at Chinese universities as responsible for attracting low-quality students, incapable of completing their degrees or having a fulfilling educational experience (Li & Song 2019). Low standards are found across all admission criteria, including the HSK exam used to assess Chinese language skills (Chai 2015). In an opinion piece published on Guancha, a Chinese online news and comments aggregator, two Chinese scholars pointed out that due to the lack of a positive selection mechanism, foreign students in China are generally from well-off families in developing countries and have limited academic drive and capabilities (Xu & Qin 2018). Drawing on his own teaching experience, a professor at Minzu Univeristy recalls that "some foreign students have trouble writing a coherent article, and some can't even understand exam questions in Chinese" (Tian 2019).

These quality gaps in admission standards may in part result from conflicting motives for higher educational internationalization embraced by different actors. Whereas the government emphasizes Chinese-language and cultural training as a way of shaping positive perceptions of China, university administrators prioritize degree enrollments to increase their revenues (Wang & Curdt-Christiansen 2016). In the past several years, the Chinese authorities at the highest levels have begun to address issues of quality assurance in foreign students' admissions. In 2018, the Ministry of Education (2018) put forth the Higher Education Quality Standard for International Students in China (Provisional), advocating the establishment of a comprehensive management system, setting up reasonable exams and assessments, and recruiting international students with academic abilities and development potential. More recently, the CCP Party Group of the Ministry of Education (2020) published a notice addressed to university party committees, stressing not to "blindly pursue globalization measures and the scale of foreign students." At the 2021 Two Sessions Meeting, a member of the CPPCC National Committee, Gao Yanming, has proposed recruiting "high-level, high-quality" international students instead of overlooking quality for the sake of quantity (Yanming, cited in Zhong 2021). Whether these statements and policies have had an effect will require future investigations.

The Future of Education as a Soft Power Mechanism

Educational exchanges and trainings make up an important and yet for now a largely overlooked facet of China's soft power. In the coming years, China's efforts at attracting students and dignitaries for exchanges and education opportunities are only likely to grow, especially in the developing world. At the latest Forum on China-African Cooperation (FOCAC) meeting, in 2018, Xi Jinping has pledged 50,000 Chinese Government Scholarships as well as 50,000 new training opportunities. Following the 2018 China-CELAC Forum, the Ministry of Foreign Affairs published a collaborative action plan, promising 6,000 government scholarships to the community of Latin American and Caribbean countries.

The implications of China's international student exchanges for its soft power mission are mixed. On the one hand, unlike CIs and Chinese state media that suffer from ideological linkages with authoritarianism and communism, education exchanges seem to be perceived in more politically neutral terms. Many students and especially short-term visitors from developing countries come away from these trips with appreciation of China and more readiness to shape their countries' policies in favor of China engagement. This suggests that perhaps taking foreigners to China and letting them experience Chinese hospitality and modernity is more effective than telling the story of China via official channels. Presenting targeted practical benefits to recipients also might be a promising strategy in shaping their perceptions. At the same time, China's higher education offerings are marked by their mixed quality that hurts the potential returns on soft power. Namely, these academic experiences are rooted in a Chinese pedagogical approach that prioritizes top-down interactions, overshadowed by underlying racial frictions, and undermined by the relatively nonselective admission criteria aimed at profit making rather than attracting a high caliber of students.

In a way, education exchanges most clearly illustrate the combination of hard and soft power resources and motives in China's image projection, as well the contradictions that ensue from this fusion. Chinese officials and university administrators converge in their desire to attract more international students, and yet their motivations behind it diverge and create frictions, with officials interested in soft power and administrators in maximizing revenues.

The fusion of cultural and market logics also shapes the mixed reception toward China's higher education initiatives. The elites and students who come to China on fully funded trips are likely to be more predisposed to expressing gratitude and leave with a positive impression, as they embrace these journeys as gifts from the Chinese government. Self-funded foreign students, on the other hand, might be at once attracted by China's low-cost offerings and more discerning of their quality, as they treat education as an investment rather than as a gift. As most foreign students in China are self-funded, the market logic likely dominates their overall evaluation of the education experience. In fact, if education quality is seen as unsatisfying, foreign students still find a way to use it to advance their careers. Some African students make up for the disappointing academic experience in China by engaging in trade (Haugen 2013). Others, use Chinese education as a steppingstone to other educational destinations, like Europe, Canada, and the United States where they hope to pursue further studies. This, of course, may change over time if China improves its education standards and makes its universities more competitive and selective.

Perhaps the larger and the more complex issue to resolve when it comes to the quality of the education experience is that of racial discrimination. The dramatic crisis that took place in the African community in Guangzhou in April 2020 when many African residents were left homeless as part of the local government's battle to control for imported COVID cases, is a manifestation of how deep-rooted racial prejudices are in Chinese society, and how they can sabotage China's efforts at building up its soft power. The evictions of Africans in Guangzhou were documented on social media, leading some African leaders to publicly summon Chinese ambassadors to account for China's actions. While the crisis mainly focused on evictions, African students also reported unfair treatment during the pandemic. A student from Botswana, for instance, shared that unlike other international students, she and other Africans had to undergo coronavirus testing, and another student complained about unequal hospital care and public transport access during the pandemic (Lau 2020). The events in Guangzhou also sparked a debate about racism among African students in China (Olander 2020), who shared their routine experiences of interacting with Chinese people. While officially, the rhetoric of China-Africa friendship has resumed on both sides, unofficially these racial tensions are unlikely to dissipate, especially at the societal level. My analysis of social media debates about this incident, for instance, found many Chinese commentators were disappointed that the government hadn't reacted more swiftly to control the African community. Mitigating routine racialized experiences of African visitors and students would require a more systemic and profound conversation about race in China. For now, there is an acknowledgment of education quality concerns by higher officials in China, but the issue of race and racism is largely obscured in official statements about China's friendship with Africa and with the Global South. How racialized tensions impact China's educational soft power efforts, especially in the developing world, is something to watch closely in the years to come.

5 Performing Public Diplomacy Spectacles

This section examines China's staging of expensive cultural spectacles catered toward global and domestic audience. The rise of global China has coincided with its hosting of a range of spectacles, including carnival-like "mega" events (Muller 2015), such as the 2008 Beijing Olympics and the 2010 Shanghai World Expo, as well as recurring diplomatic summits like FOCAC and various BRI events, and more recently a range of smaller, micro-spectacles like trade fairs and economic summits that carry a public diplomacy component.

It is helpful to distinguish between global mega events that involve a competitive international selection process and China-initiated spectacles that originate in China and take place on a smaller scale. As for the former, the two key events are the Beijing Olympics and the Shanghai World Expo. In competing for both, China took part in a rigorous selection process that took massive investments and years of intensive preparation. The Beijing Olympics cost the government more than $28 billion (*The Guardian* 2008) and involved controversial policies, such as the relocation of about 1.5 million people out of Beijing. The Shanghai 2010 World Expo cost an estimated $44 billion and similarly involved massive relocation of families and factories (Barboza 2010). Both events attracted unprecedented audiences. The Beijing Games drew in 4.7 billion television viewers between August 8 and August 25, 2008 (Nielsen 2008), and the Shanghai Expo attracted more than 73 million visitors from 246 countries (Bloomberg News 2010). Both events positioned China at the heart of the international community.

In addition to these spectacular global events, the Chinese government has initiated its own diplomatic spectacles – more routine events focused on economic diplomacy. The number of regional and global summits in China has mushroomed in the past two decades. Some of these initiatives, such as FOCAC, date back to 2000 when China restarted its vigorous relationship with the African continent. More recently, the Chinese government has launched new strategic regional forums, including the China-CELAC forum (The Community of Latin American and Caribbean States) in 2015, and the China–Central Asia Cooperation Forum in 2012. The BRI initiative also gave rise to a number of summits, including the BRI Forum that brings participants from more than 150 countries, as well as a series of smaller summits, such as the Belt and Road International Youth Forum that regularly convenes 100 participants from 30 countries. These summits combine economic deals and major investment announcements with elite networking and cultural performances and tours of China.

In addition to major summit diplomacy, China has also initiated a number of its own trade expos. Some, such as the 2018 China International Import Expo, are aimed at global audiences and participants. Others, such as the 2019 China-Africa Economic and Trade Expo held in Changsha, Hunan province, target specific regions. As with economic summits, these are not just business events but are also important public diplomacy platforms. International trade expos attract officials, journalists, as well as entrepreneurs, and tend to facilitate large-scale economic deals alongside smaller people-to-people interactions.

This section explores the workings of China's public diplomacy spectacles by examining the motives behind them, as well as their varied implementation and implications for the party-state's domestic and international legitimacy. Much of the discussion will focus on the most dramatic global mega events, the Beijing Olympics and the Shanghai Expo as they present the starkest illustrations of Chinese soft power, but examples from other China-initiated events are also included here. The analysis that follows explains the entwined international and domestic motivations behind the staging of mega events and public diplomacy spectacles. The section further explores the contested nature of mega events when it comes to China's soft power projections internationally and domestically. Whereas the party-state uses these events as a platform for projecting a positive international image and for molding civilized and cosmopolitan citizens, other actors, including global civil society, media, and Chinese citizens, take advantage of these staged acts to challenge and reinvent the official narratives. This is especially notable for the major international events, but the contestation theme is also present in smaller, China-initiated public spectacles.

International and Domestic: Parallel Motivations Behind Diplomatic Spectacles

In contrast to other soft power initiatives that tend to feature more strongly the external political motivations of the party-state, when it comes to hosting public diplomacy spectacles, international and domestic rationales are equally significant. As for external motivations, hosting major diplomatic events, especially the competitive ones, like the Olympics and the World Expo, has historically been associated with international prestige. The modern Olympic Games – the world's leading sports event dating back to 1896 – embodies the missions of peace building and universalism, as well as competition for global status. Similarly to its competitors and predecessors, Beijing has persisted in its bid to host the games as a way of promoting China's political and diplomatic agenda and gaining legitimacy in the international community (Li 2013).

The World Expo dates back to 1851 and is known as a highly prestigious event that some experts describe as "arguably the single biggest showcasing event of a nation outside of its borders" (Wang 2020). Host countries are selected every year through a rigorous competition administered by the Bureau International des Expositions (BIE) general assembly. Yang Jiechi (2010), then China's foreign minister, asserted that the Shanghai Expo "promotes China's friendly cooperation with various countries in all aspects, and immensely enriches the essence of China's diplomacy in the new era."

The official ceremonies of mega events that show off China to the world further demonstrate the importance of external soft power motives. The Beijing

Olympics, for instance, presented Chinese culture as harmonious with and equal to that of the West, with cultural ceremonies highlighting the historic achievements and inventions of the Chinese civilization that contributed to the development of the West (Collins 2008). The Opening Ceremony also showed off China's technological progress through the use of sophisticated technologies and the display of major Chinese tech companies as contributors to the event, as well as the impressive Olympic facilities. China, therefore, used the Olympics as an opportune strategy "to educate the world about modern China" (Cull 2008, p. 135), and to demonstrate its "economic, technological, cultural, social and environmental achievements to the rest of the world" (Latham 2009, p. 25).

The Shanghai Expo also combined the themes of tradition and modernity in introducing China's prowess to foreign visitors. In describing the China pavilion, the designer, He Jingtang, highlights that "every element used in the China Pavilion has its Chinese origin. ... It's an abstract expression of China's 5,000 years of history and the culture of 56 ethnic groups" (He Jingtang, cited in Wang 2010). Hu Jintao introduced the exhibit as "showcasing the glorious accomplishments of the 60 years of New China, especially the 30 years since Reform and Opening Up" (Hu Jintao, cited in Xinhua News Agency 2010).

External communication is also part of smaller China-initiated spectacles. For instance, regional economic summits such as FOCAC, symbolize to

Figure 3 Night view of the Expo Axis and China Pavilion at the Shanghai Expo 2010 (Tomlelouch / Getty Images)

Africa as well as to the world at large China's growing influence and engage-ment with the continent. Smaller events at the provincial level also incorporate a public diplomacy component. At the 2016 Hunan-Ethiopia Investment Cooperation Matchmaking Event, for instance, then governor of Hunan Xu Dazhe emphasized that the cooperation "reflects the rising heat of the Hunan-Ethiopia strategic and cooperative relationship and indicates a bright future for friendly cooperation between Hunan and Ethiopia in all aspects" (Xu Dazhe, cited in Liu 2017b). More recently, in November 2020, at the China (Henan)-Switzerland Industrial Promotion Event, Yin Hong, the governor of Henan, promoted his province and highlighted its impressive capacity in controlling the pandemic, which was conducive to attracting foreign invest-ments (*People's Daily* 2020).

At the same time, Chinese authorities deployed a variety of techniques to turn these events into domestic educational and civilizing platforms. Prior to the Beijing Olympics, an extensive Olympic education program was launched to expand students' international perspective in addition to shaping their "Olympic spirit" in preparation for the games (Brownell 2009) through English classes, etiquette training, and volunteerism (Brady 2009b). The official propaganda posters also combined the spirited call for supporting the Olympics with an emphasis on the importance of "good manners," including directives on appropriate ways of taking public transport and withdrawing money, among other activities (de Kloet et al. 2008).

The Shanghai Expo also clearly featured a domestic agenda. The event served an important pedagogical function of teaching Chinese citizens about "how to understand the national self through a shared vision of Chinese greatness, past, present, and future" introduced at the China pavilion (Hubbert 2017, p. 51). Outside the venue, messages targeted domestic audiences to attend the Expo. "See the world without leaving the country," read a billboard sign at the Shanghai Hongqiao Airport (Dynon 2014). The majority of attendants of the Shanghai Expo were Chinese citizens (Barboza 2010).

The domestic motives are also apparent in summit diplomacy and in smaller trade expos. Though diplomatic summits aren't open to the general public, they are widely broadcast domestically. In covering the 2018 FOCAC summit, Chinese state media used the event to extol Xi Jinping's leadership. *China News* employed the headline of "Xi Jinping's 'Beijing Time' of FOCAC" (Zhang 2018), and Xinhua (2018) published the full text of Xi Jinping's keynote speech at the opening ceremony. The trade expos draw in thousands of local participants. The 2019 China-Africa Trade Expo in Changsha, for instance, attracted more than 100,000 visitors (Yang & Zhang 2019) – most of them from Changsha.

Figure 4 Chinese visitors lining up to enter the 2019 China-Africa Trade Expo in Changsha, Hunan (Maria Repnikova)

The international and domestic motives in the case of public diplomacy spectacles, therefore, appear to fuse and complement each other. They at once project China's rise to international publics and actors, as well as aim to spark patriotism and mold more disciplined and worldly citizens.

The Implications of Public Diplomacy Spectacles for China's Soft Power

China's ability to host such high-stakes global events as the Olympics is arguably already a win for its global image, and yet these events also open up opportunities for international and domestic actors to deploy them for a selective agenda that doesn't always fit with that of China's soft power. Overall, China's success is more apparent domestically, but even there, there is subtle contestation and critique of official norms and values afforded by mega spectacles.

International Implications

In thinking about the implications of hosting mega events for China's global image, it is important to recognize the "inherent instability about great events that makes them subject to capture in surprising and unanticipated ways" (Price 2008, p. 6). The Beijing Olympics was certainly "captured" by a variety of actors. In reporting on the games, Western journalists, for instance, were preoccupied with uncovering the "real China" that's hidden in China's official narratives (Latham 2009). In the run up to the Olympics, Western media reported on governance and societal costs of the games, including forced evictions (Borger 2007) and political crackdowns (Yardley 2008). Days after the impressive Opening Ceremony, foreign journalists also uncovered its inauthentic features, such as the computer animation behind the fireworks and the "fake" singing at the ceremony (Kent 2008; Watts 2008). The Chinese organizers presented a nine-year-old, Lin Miaoke, as the singer of the national anthem, but it turned out that the real voice belonged to seven-year-old Yang Peiyi whose crooked teeth made her a less photogenic performer. "The country's quest for perfection apparently includes children," reported NBC News (AP 2008). "The dedication to authenticity apparently does not extend to Olympics ceremonies," wrote ABC News (Kent 2008).

Global civil society, Western celebrities and athletes, among other actors, used the Beijing Olympics to pressure China to act on the Darfur genocide. The damaging "Darfur Olympics" label has emerged, as China's decision not to condemn the genocide and to continue to economically collaborate with Sudanese elites was depicted as immoral. A popular op-ed authored by Mia

and Ronan Farrow (2007) accused China of "bankrolling" genocide by continuing to buy Sudanese oil despite the revelations of massive human rights abuses.
Pro-Tibetan demonstrators also used the Olympic torch ceremony to shame
China on its human rights violations in Tibet. Some of these protests even
turned violent, leading to arrests, and forcing Western politicians to publicly
address China's human rights record.

This contestation or capture of the Beijing Olympics was in part a product of
opportune circumstances, but it was also provoked by China's own top-down
approach to staging mega events and instigated by Western civil society and
media biases about China. In contrast to the London Olympics that were
coordinated by the government but allowed for input and participation of
diverse entities, Beijing's "elitist" and "center-driven" approach gave rise to
international suspicions of its intentions (Li 2013, p. 1725). The Chinese
government's media policy of combining temporary openings for more extensive Western coverage with a tightened control over domestic media only made
China appear more as an "authoritarian 'other'" (Smith 2008).

The Chinese government's handling of Western media critiques and civil
society accusations further featured a defensive tone that only provoked more
agitation. In response to Western media investigations of China's domestic
governance failures, for instance, Chinese state media attacked Western journalists as "not understanding the 'real China'" (Latham 2009, p. 34). In
response to accusations about Darfur, Chinese officials emphasized that an
economic-focused approach in Sudan is as valid as the Western emphasis on
human rights (Hubbert 2014). In addressing the pro-Tibetan demonstrators,
Wang Hui, the head of the Department of News and Publicity of the Beijing
Olympic Organizing Committee, accused them of offending the Olympic spirit
(Wang 2008).

At the same time, biased dispositions and narratives of Western actors about
China also played into the tensions during the Beijing Olympics. Instead of
attempting to construct a new narrative about China, many Western civil society
and media actors largely embraced the Cold War ideological narrative, and with
that ended up sparking more Chinese nationalism (Finley & Xin 2010). Rather
than using the torch relay as an opportunity for dialogue, for instance, "these
groups allowed their causes to be integrated into a growing anti-China movement in the West" (Finley & Xin 2010, p. 882). This anti-China sentiment was
likely also amplified by China's unwillingness to conform to the West, in
contrast to Japan and Korea, which adopted the narratives and images accept-
able to the West in their Olympic ceremonies (Collins 2011).

The other major mega event – the Shanghai World Expo – didn't get as derailed
by international messaging as the Beijing Olympics, and yet it also featured some

international controversies. Thirty-eight human rights groups accused the Chinese government of massive human rights violations in forcefully evicting 18,000 families for the sake of the expo. Human Rights Watch also publicized police raids on homes of famous Shanghai activists prior to the expo.

Overall, if we take a more long-term view on these global mega events, it is unclear whether they managed to shift global public opinion in favor of China. On the one hand, Pew public opinion surveys found that in 2009 and 2011 following China's hosting of the Beijing Olympics and the Shanghai Expo, unfavorable views of China declined in some countries, like the United States, Germany, and Japan (Pew Research Center 2009, 2011). Notably, countries in the Global South began to "view China as more of a partner to their country" the year after the Beijing Olympics (Pew Research Center 2009). At the same time, these gains are relatively minor, at least in the Western contexts where views of China have remained consistently negative (Silver et al. 2020).

Ironically, despite being less costly and less globally visible than mega events, China-initiated public diplomacy spectacles, such as economic summits, might actually have a more sustained effect on its soft power in the long run. They are less prone to international controversy. The routine nature of these events, with some summits taking place annually, is also conducive to elite network formation and promotion of China's interests (Benabdallah 2020). The soft power effect in this case might be less perceptible, and yet more significant for China's BRI policy and for building legitimacy in the Global South.

Domestic Context: A Mix of Nationalism and Subtle Contestation

Domestically, staging mass events and public diplomacy spectacles has resulted in a mix of nationalism and societal contestation that pierced through grand festivities. As for nationalistic sentiments, these events were a celebration of China's success story. The Olympic Games, in particular, "were a triumphant symbol of the great progress their country and economy had achieved over the recent years" (Manzenreiter 2010, p. 42). According to public opinion research conducted by Fudan University, 92.8 percent of respondents thought of the Expo as positively influencing the development of Shanghai (Fudan University Media and Public Opinion Research Center 2010, cited in Cao 2010).

It is challenging to decipher public opinion about routine public diplomacy spectacles and trade fairs, but these types of events also appeal to a nationalistic sentiment. Public diplomacy events, like FOCAC, as noted earlier, are widely broadcast in domestic media, highlighting China's prowess and leadership in the developing world. Trade expos are also mediatized and are popular with Chinese residents. Many find attending trade expos entertaining or a way to pass time. The author's experience at the Hunan China-Africa trade expo in 2019 found local attendants drawn more to domestic exhibits and products and more eager to "consume" China as part of this experience.

At the same time, mega events also serve as platforms for different Chinese groups and actors to redefine national identity and their modes of belonging. At the Shanghai Expo, Chinese citizen intellectuals – both within and outside the system – promoted alternative visions of "harmony" to the official and corporate presentations (Callahan 2012). Jia Zhangke's film, *Shanghai Legends*, officially commissioned by and shown at the Expo, for instance, countered the official theme of harmony by featuring different individuals as "loners" and subtly critiquing China's traditional family structure. Cai Guoqiang's exhibit outside of the official Expo presented an alternative narrative to that of celebrating China's urbanization – a narrative channeled at the Expo – by recognizing rural life and creativity. These artist-intellectuals do not directly oppose the state but, rather, engage in "multiplying and decentering China's dreams" (Callahan 2012, p. 264).

At the Beijing Olympics, Chinese intellectuals and students took advantage of the "commodity spectacle" to redefine their way of belonging in the Chinese state, including sentiments of unity, as well as contestation and resentment (Hubbert 2010). Chinese intellectuals promoted the cultural significance of *laozihao* (traditional Chinese cultural products) as a way of applying their cultural knowledge to serve the nation and thereby created a renewed sense of belonging or assimilation in the Chinese state (Hubbert 2010). At the same time, some students and intellectuals critiqued the avant-garde Olympic architecture as inauthentic and out of place, subtly attributing responsibility to the state for endorsing and implementing these projects. Forced evictions – the more contentious human rights violation in preparation for the Beijing Olympics – were met with more explicit and fiercer pushback. Some Beijing residents expressed resistance by writing "Oppose forced eviction" and "Where are our rights?" on windows and banners and refused to leave their homes for more than a year (*The New York Times* 2007).

Looking Ahead: The Future of Public Diplomacy Spectacles

Public diplomacy spectacles will remain an important component of China's soft power. The trends presented in this section, including international and some domestic contestation surrounding these events, as well as the domestic nationalistic appeal of public diplomacy spectacles will likely feature in the events to come. As for mega events, while scholars are still analyzing the 2008 Beijing Olympics, China is about to host its second Olympics – the 2022 Beijing

Winter Games. In comparison to the 2008 Olympics, the upcoming games will stir even more controversy. On the one hand, it's a chance for China to show off its successful coronavirus recovery, as well as its ascendance to great power status with winning the bid to host the Olympics twice in the same city. At the same time, the international condemnation of the games is already widespread. Whereas in 2008, the divisive issue was China's reluctance to condemn the Darfur genocide, this time the discourse has shifted to claims of genocide within China's borders, in Xinjiang. The slogan "Genocide Olympics" has been resurrected by the World Uyghur Congress, and more than 160 human rights groups around the world have called for a global boycott of the Beijing Olympics. The 2022 games are also likely to attract more global attention to political tightening across China's civil society space. As the Olympics already come at a time when China's favorability has declined across major industrialized economies due to the negative associations with China's handling of the coronavirus outbreak in Wuhan (Silver et al. 2020), the external soft power gains, especially in the developed world, are likely to be modest. Much, of course, rests on the response by the Chinese government, but thus far what we see are more defensive statements, echoing those from 2008.

Aside from mega events, the Chinese government will continue to practice economic summit diplomacy. These routine, more contained public diplomacy spectacles are more promising for China's soft power. Other than gaining international recognition, China has now also set international norms when it comes to summit diplomacy. The FOCAC, for instance, has spurred similar efforts from other regional powers. The European Union launched the Africa-EU Strategic Partnership in 2007, and Russia hosted its inaugural Africa summit in 2019.

The routine nature of economic summits and trade expos also allows for some evolution and learning over time. Different themes emerge at different economic summits. At this year's FOCAC meeting that took place in Senegal on November 29–30, 2021, for instance, the focus was on the most urgent areas of concern for the African continent, including vaccine cooperation, economic recovery, and transformative development. Following some pushback at the 2017 BRI summit, China's BRI diplomacy has now readjusted to include environmental protections alongside major economic deals.

At the same time, these summits, rooted primarily in shared economic interests, are also starting to encounter some pushback. Six Eastern European countries did not send their top leaders to the China-led 2021 "17+1 Summit" – a forum launched in 2012 aimed at building ties with Eastern Europe. The reason was competing security considerations under Biden administration as well as distrust in China's ability to deliver on its economic offerings (Lau 2021). It remains to be seen, therefore, how China-led bilateral and regional summits will survive into the future. As with China's other soft power mechanisms, for both mega events and regional economic summits and expos, it may prove that China's success will be more apparent in the Global South where China faces less direct competition from other major powers and where it delivers more tangible economic benefits.

The envisioned domestic gains from hosting public diplomacy spectacles, especially mega events, but also trade expos and summits, however, mean that the Chinese government will continue to invest heavily in these initiatives regardless of international setbacks. While mega events incite some subtle contestation, the overarching sentiment that emerges from these events is that of national unity and pride. The news about China's winning the bid to host the 2022 Winter Olympics was met with jubilation across the country. As soon as the win was announced, thousands of people gathered at the Beijing Olympic Park burst into cheers, and the celebration culminated as everyone sang "Ode to the Motherland" together (Han 2015). The "2022 Winter Olympic" hashtag has now generated more than 88 million reads and more than 100,000 discussion posts on Weibo (Weibo hashtag topic "2022 Winter Olympic"). Summit and expo diplomacy has also helped showcase China's emerging role as the global savior, especially in light of its coronavirus diplomacy in the Global South. Chinese media proudly reports on the 2021 FOCAC summit held in Senegal: "Constructing a Stronger China-Africa Community with a Shared Future in the Post-Pandemic Era" (He 2021). These widely mediatized public diplomacy spectacles stoke the fire of the growing domestic nationalism under Xi Jinping. As such, we can anticipate seeing a proliferation of these events and China's continued quest to project its global status through symbolic influence of a mass spectacle.

6 Conclusions and Future Directions

This Element illustrated China's distinctive notions and practices of soft power. Chinese experts and officials have embraced, reinvented, and expanded the concept of soft power originally coined by Joseph Nye. In contrast to clear distinctions made between hard and soft power in Nye's works, Chinese writings advocate for fluid boundaries between hard and soft power, treating them as symbiotic and mutually empowering. Whereas Nye put forward three key sources of soft power – culture, values, and foreign policy – Chinese interpretations tend to place an emphasis on the cultural dimension, and yet culture encompasses an ambiguous category that combines traditional culture with ideology, history, morality, and even economic governance. Some Chinese thinkers further propose political capacity and developmental experiences and practices as additional sources of China's soft power. Finally, whereas the Western understanding of soft power tends to prioritize external audiences, Chinese motivations for soft power are rooted as much domestically as internationally. In particular, soft power is associated with political stability and societal cohesion.

The analysis of the workings of the core Chinese soft power instruments, including Confucius Institutes, international media, education exchanges, and public diplomacy spectacles, reflects some of these visions. The motivations for expanding most soft power channels, for instance, feature a mix of domestic and international considerations. In some soft power channels, such as public spectacles, this combination is especially apparent. In others, like education, media, and Confucius Institutes, domestic factors are more subtle, yet still notable. Internationalization of Chinese media and higher education institutions is associated with new markets and revenues for Chinese media enterprises and universities. Expansion of CIs presents a cultural exposure opportunity to foreign students but also to Chinese teachers and volunteers.

The fusion of hard and in particular material power and cultural power is also notable in the implementation of the core soft power initiatives. For instance, pragmatic incentives, such as job opportunities associated with speaking Chinese language, entice at least some students to enroll in Confucius Institutes. Chinese media and communication infrastructure is appealing in large part because it is accessible and less costly than alternative options. Chinese higher education has seen a dramatic rise in international students in part because of its affordability and large-scale scholarships offered by the Chinese government. Chinese public spectacles, like major diplomatic summits and trade expos, tend to lure in participants as much with economic deals as with cultural offerings.

The analysis of the implementation of Chinese soft power further reveals its deliberate decentralization. Unlike the frequent popular portrayals of Chinese soft power as orchestrated from the top-down, in reality, these initiatives feature significant localization – something encouraged by authorities in Beijing. The Confucius Institutes are comanaged by local and Chinese directors and actively adjust their practices to local contexts. Chinese media deliberately hire local journalists and distribute their content via local media outlets. Chinese universities take their own initiatives in attracting international students, and Chinese provincial leaders are increasingly embracing public diplomacy via trade expos and other public events that are not coordinated by the central government. This decentralized mode of implementation is associated with both the innovative and adaptive nature of Chinese soft power, as well as with its mixed and often unpredictable quality.

One of the major and perhaps most contested themes explored in this Element is the effectiveness of Chinese soft power initiatives. The preceding sections reveal some variation across regions, as well as soft power instruments. As for regions, overall, Chinese soft power tactics appear to be more appealing in the Global South. The popular associations between Chinese soft power offerings and China's autocratic political system, for instance, are still present but less pronounced in Africa where practical enticements of Chinese soft power offerings can overpower ideological concerns. Whereas in major industrialized nations, views of China have become more negative over time, reaching a historical low in the summer of 2020 (Silver et al. 2020), views of China in Africa and in Latin America have been more favorable (Silver et al. 2020). A 2019/2020 Afrobarometer research report, for instance, shows that the majority of respondents in African countries perceive Chinese influence as "mostly positive," though these positive views have slightly decreased compared with 2014/2015 (Sanny and Selormey 2020). As for variation across instruments, the more experiential soft power channels, like education and training exchanges, appear to be more effective in shifting perceptions about China than the more indirect and politicized channels, like Chinese media that are not trusted by publics across regional contexts. Unpacking implications of Chinese soft power, however, is still in the early stages of research, presenting an exciting opportunity for future scholarship.

Future Research Directions

Explaining the Varied Motivations and Practices of Chinese Soft Power

To better grapple with the elusive and somewhat contradictory effects and implications of Chinese soft power initiatives, our research efforts can focus more on untangling how they work across different cultural and political contexts. This means a move away from largely testing China's soft power performance by applying Nye's concept to China to an engagement in grounded theory building, whereby China's initiatives are analyzed on their own terms. Methodologically, an ethnographic or a fieldwork-oriented approach that shifts our focus from the study of assets or narratives and toward the study of practices or cultural encounters is especially useful. Several exemplary works in the field already embrace this approach, including Hubbert's (2019) study of Confucius

Institutes in the United States, Gagliardone and Pal's (2017) work on Chinese journalists in Africa, Umejei's work (2018) on African journalists at Chinese media enterprises, and Haugen's (2013) analysis of African students in China, among other examples. Building on these studies, scholars of Chinese soft power can connect the macro analysis of official discourse and policies with the micro or granular analysis of varied motivations and practices of different participants in China's soft power initiatives. How different actors envision their roles in the soft power project and how that shapes their relative contributions are significant for expanding our understanding of how China's soft power works.

In my analysis of Chinese soft power in Africa, and specifically in Ethiopia, I find that different actors derive their own benefits and visions from this project, often as distinct from the official agenda promoted by Beijing. Whereas the Chinese government tends to emphasize altruism and solidarity with African nations, Chinese teachers at Confucius Institutes tend to be attracted by professional empowerment and career advancement, and Chinese trainers who train African elites are driven more by the bureaucratic obligations of "showing off" China than by the quest to build deeper connections or solidarities. These conflicting motivations between high-level visionaries in Beijing and individuals who are tasked with carrying out China's soft power project tend to affect the quality of the cultural encounter. Chinese teachers and trainers pay less attention to building meaningful connections and friendships than to fulfilling their own professional and bureaucratic obligations.

Motivations for experiencing China's soft power are also varied on the receiving side. While many studies reveal the mixed and often negative reception toward Chinese soft power initiatives, we know less about what draws some participants to engage with China's offerings in the first place. In my interviews with Ethiopian elites, students, and journalists, I find that many of these individuals take advantage of China's tangible offerings, including the opportunities to travel and experience China, to secure employment through the Chinese language, and to disseminate a more positive image of Ethiopia through China's global media outlets, among other incentives. To what extent this participation yields admiration for China in the long term is questionable, but it does appear to facilitate a sentiment of inspiration and curiosity, even if fears and anxieties about China's involvement with Ethiopia coexist with these positive impressions. Grasping these layered motivations and sentiments requires stepping beyond public opinion surveys or interview questions that directly target respondents' sentiments about China and asking about what China and its offerings signify for the participants.

Chinese Soft Power in a Comparative Context

The study of China's soft power can also be significantly enriched with more comparative work. In particular, we need to shift from essentializing China or emphasizing the uniqueness of its global pursuits, including soft power, and place China's initiatives in a wider comparative context. Such work has been done effectively in the study of China's global capital, with Lee's (2017) transformative book demonstrating that, counterintuitively, Chinese capital in Zambia has been more adaptive or accommodating to local pressures than global private capital, in particular in the case of the copper-mining sector. When it comes to soft power, the particularity of China's political system appears to dissuade scholars from doing comparative work and instead leads them to stress China's ideological constraints or the challenge for China's authoritarian system in captivating international publics. It is only through comparative contextualization, however, that we can decipher which facets of China's soft power are distinctive, and which are more generalizable, as well as how China's performance fares in comparison with other major powers.

The comparison between China and the United States can be particularly illuminating as the two powers tend to perceive each other as the core competitors for soft power in the international system. My initial analysis of Chinese and US soft power initiatives in Ethiopia, including cultural centers and state-sponsored media operations, helps interrogate some assumptions about Chinese soft power. First, I find that whereas China's soft power is often associated with ideological brainwashing, the emphasis on ideology or political values is more apparent in the case of the United States than that of China, with China adopting a more depoliticized and pragmatic approach in attracting local publics. Whereas the United States continues to deliberately integrate democratic values and practices into its cultural engagements, China emphasizes tangible or material opportunities. Second, the comparative analysis shows that China's practice of soft power is heavily shaped by American influence, with China adopting some techniques and materials from the United States in the presentation of its own image. The materials used in training seminars with African elites, for instance, often feature citations from American academics and publications, and even some of the core ideas "transferred" in these seminars are borrowed from American business schools. Chinese soft power, therefore, is both distinctive in its offerings but also hybrid or Westernized. These initial contrasts can be tested in other cases where Chinese and US interests compete, including in Latin America, the Caribbean, and Eastern Europe, among other contexts. Other fruitful comparisons could be drawn between China and major authoritarian countries, like Russia, as well as between China and South Korea or Japan, which share some cultural similarities but different modes of soft power projection.

Another productive comparison to pursue is that of China's soft power operations across economic, cultural, and political contexts. Comparisons between China's soft power operations in developed versus developing countries can be insightful in revealing to what extent economic dependencies on China shape the influence of its cultural outreach. In Ethiopia, I find that China's cultural initiatives are associated with economic opportunities, and yet the suspicions and fears of China's economic power can also translate into reluctance to embrace Chinese culture and build personal ties. It would be interesting to see whether and how such contradictions play out in more developed contexts where there is still significant economic dependency on China but also more leverage to push back, and where China's economic offerings might be less alluring to local publics.

A cross-cultural comparison could reveal whether and how cultural similarities and differences may play into the resonance of China's soft power initiatives. Are China's cultural initiatives relatively more popular in East Asia than they are in Africa or Russia, or does the cultural factor not carry much significance given the pragmatic offerings of Chinese soft power? A cross-political system comparison would show whether the type of political system matters for reception toward China's soft power initiatives. Specifically, given the emphasis in the literature on weak legitimacy of China's political system as hurting its soft power pursuits, it would be interesting to examine whether China's initiatives are more popular in authoritarian versus democratic contexts. Such research would also help untangle and investigate the popular claims that China is exporting its authoritarian model and building an illiberal world order through its soft power pursuits.

Exploring New Instruments of China's Soft Power

Parallel to deepening our understanding of the most prominent, state-sponsored instruments of China's soft power discussed in this Element, we should explore less apparent but still potentially significant channels of China's image construction, including via Chinese diaspora, as well as Chinese companies and NGOs. As for the role of diaspora, future studies could examine how diaspora communities serve as a linkage for, a target of, and an impediment for China's soft power campaigns. The importance of Chinese diaspora as a connecting bridge is most evident in the context of China's media outreach. We already know that local Chinese-language media can facilitate content distribution agreements for China's state-owned media outlets (Sun 2010b). More studies into this brokerage function of Chinese language media could help us better understand the diverse localization practices of China's state media outlets.

Chinese diasporic communities, of course, are also a target of China's external propaganda campaigns – something that scholars and policymakers primarily associate with the work of the United Front Department and China's sharp power that involves financial co-optation and coercive practices (Brady 2017). While it's easy to dismiss or to frame CCP's diasporic outreach efforts as a form of sharp power, this ignores· the importance of enticement in Chinese official efforts especially with regard to more transient groups like Chinese overseas students. For instance, the Chinese Government Award for Outstanding Self-Financed Students Abroad was established in 2003 to recognize overseas students with exceptional academic performance (Xinhua News Agency 2019). The Chinese government also offers great incentives for overseas students to start their own businesses upon returning home. As of 2018, there were 351 entrepreneurship parks in China, which house more than 23,000 companies and have attracted 86,000 overseas returnees (Xu 2018). Considering the stress placed on building "cultural confidence" and national cohesiveness in China's soft power narratives discussed in Section 1, studying how the Chinese government shapes the sentiments of overseas Chinese publics, especially students who are likely to return to China, should fall under our future research agenda on China's global soft power operations. This doesn't dismiss the presence of coercive instruments but calls for a broader understanding of official diasporic outreach.

Other than a bridge and a target, diasporic communities can also serve as a hindrance for China's image work. In recent years, the frictions between China's migrant communities and local communities have attracted media attention in places like Kenya (Goldstein 2018), Kazakhstan (Jardine 2019), and Malaysia (Sukumaran 2019), among other countries. The Chinese government also often blames local Chinese communities for jeopardizing the image of the Chinese state by engaging in illicit behavior like corruption and prostitution (Zhao 2017). How Chinese embassies mitigate these frictions and how Chinese migrant communities affect the perceptions of local publics about China are fascinating issues to explore in the context of China's soft power goals.

Finally, the role of Chinese enterprises (both state owned and private) and Chinese civil society (NGOs) are important to integrate into future analyses of China's global soft power. As Chinese companies continue to expand overseas, it will be interesting to examine whether and how they brand themselves in local communities, and how perceptions of Chinese company operations feed into the views on Chinese government and Chinese culture. Following in the footsteps of other Chinese actors, like media and CIs, Chinese NGOs are also increasingly expanding their operations outside their borders, especially in Africa (Hsu et al. 2016; Xie 2017). What is distinctive about these NGO practices in contrast to Western civil society operations and how their work plays into China's soft power in the developing world are fascinating areas of study.

Bibliography

Barboza, D. (2010). Shanghai Expo Sets Record with 73 Million Visitors, www
.nytimes.com/2010/11/03/world/asia/03shanghai.html.

Bai, Y. (2014). International Chinese Language Teaching Materials Walking
into a New Age – Deputy Director of National Hanban Xia Jianhui Discusses
the Development of Chinese Language Materials [国际汉语教材走进新时
代–国家汉办副主任夏建辉谈汉语教材发展], http://world.people.com.cn
/n/2014/0418/c157278-24911449.html.

BBC News. (2018). Huawei and ZTE Handed 5G Network Can in Australia,
www.bbc.com/news/technology-45281495.

BBC News (2021). Xi Jinping Calls for More "Loveable" Image for China in
Bid to Make Friends, www.bbc.com/news/world-asia-china-57327177.

Benabdallah, L. (2020). *Shaping the Future of Power: Knowledge Production
and Network-Building in China-Africa Relations*, Ann Arbor: University of
Michigan Press.

Bley, B. (2019). *Charting China, the (Not Always) Super Power*,
www.lowyinstitute.org/the-interpreter/charting-china-not-always-super-power.

Bloomberg News. (2010). Shanghai's World Expo to Close After Hosting
Record Visitors, www.bloomberg.com/news/articles/2010-10-31/shanghai-
s-world-expo-to-close-after-attracting-record-72-million-visitors.

Bonyhady, N. & Baker, J. (2019). "Like the Alliance Francaise": Sydney Uni Boss
Defends Confucius Institute, www.smh.com.au/politics/federal/like-the-alliance-
francaise-sydney-uni-boss-defends-confucius-institute-20190826-p52kv5.html.

Borger, J. (2007). Olympics Blamed for Forcible Removal of 2 m over 20 Years,
The Guardian, www.theguardian.com/world/2007/jun/06/sport.china.

Brady, A.-M. (2015). China's Foreign Propaganda Machine. *Journal of
Democracy*, 26(4), 51–9.

Brady, A.-M. (2017). *Magic Weapons: China's Political Influence Activities
under Xi Jinping*, www.wilsoncenter.org/article/magic-weapons-chinas-
political-influence-activities-under-xi-jinping.

Brady, A.-M. (2009a). *Marketing Dictatorship: Propaganda and Thought Work
in Contemporary China*, Lanham, MD: Rowman & Littlefield.

Brady, A.-M. (2009b). The Beijing Olympics as a Campaign of Mass Distraction:
Special Section on the Beijing 2008 Olympics. *China Quarterly*, 197, 1–24.

Brazys, S. & Dukalskis, A. (2019). Rising Powers and Grassroots Image
Management: Confucius Institutes and China in the Media. *The Chinese
Journal of International Politics*, 12(4), 557–84.

Brownell, S. (2009). Beijing's Olympic Education Programme: Re-Thinking Suzhi Education, Re-Imagining an International China. *China Quarterly*, 197, 44–63.

Callahan, W. A. (2012). Shanghai's Alternative Futures: The World Expo, Citizen Intellectuals, and China's New Civil Society. *China Information*, 26 (2), 251–73.

Cao, J. (2010). Ninety five percent of People Think the Expo Was a Big Success [九成五认为世博会圆满成功], https://epaper.gmw.cn/gmrb/html/2010-11/ 01/nw.D110000gmrb_20101101_3-03.htm.

CBC News. (2019). Chinese Culture Program Removed from 18 New Brunswick Schools, www.cbc.ca/news/canada/new-brunswick/confucius-institute-programs-china-school-1.5259963.

CCP Party Group of the Ministry of Education. (2020). *Notification from CCP Party Group of the Ministry of Education about Studying and Implementing the Spirit of General Secretary Xi Jinping's Important Reply to All Pakistani Students at University of Science and Technology Beijing* [中共教育部党组 关于学习贯彻习近平总书记给北京科技大学全体巴基斯坦留学生重要 回信精神的通知], www.moe.gov.cn/srcsite/A20/s7068/202005/ t20200522_457897.html.

Center for Language Education and Cooperation, List of Projects, www.chinese.cn/page/#/pcpage/projectlist.

CGTN. (2017). Full Text of CGTN Controller Jiang Heping's Speech: Innovation and Creative Practices in the New Era, news.cgtn.com/news/ 3449444d30637a6333566d54/index.html.

CGTN. (2019). Voice Linking China & Africa: African Voice Actress Dubs Chinese Dramas to Reach African Audiences, https://news.cgtn.com/news/ 79676a4e33494464776c6d636a4e6e62684a4856/index.html.

Chai, X. (2015). Comparative Study about China and US Educational Examination Systems for International Students [中美留学生教育招生考 试体系对比研究]. *Zhongguo Kaoshi*, 5, 39–46.

Chen, X. (2020). New NGO to Operate China's Confucius Institutes, "Disperse Misinterpretation," www.globaltimes.cn/content/1193584.shtml.

Cheng, M. (2013). How to Enter the Main Field of Global Communication – Take "Russia Today" TV Station as an Example [如何进入国际传播的主阵 地–以 "今日俄罗斯(RT)" 电视台为例]. *Xinwen Yu Xiezuo*, 6, 94–5.

Cheng, M. (2018). On the External Communication of Socialist Thoughts with Chinese Characteristics [谈新时代中国特色社会主义思想的对外传播]. *Duiwai Chuanbo*, March, pp. 7–9, 29.

Chinese International Education Foundation. *Chairman Address*, www .cief.org.cn/lsczc.

Chinh, N. V. (2014). Confucius Institutes in the Mekong Region: China's Soft Power or Soft Border? *Issues and Studies; Taipei*, 50(4), 85–117.

Collins, S. (2008). The Fragility of Asian National Identity in the Olympic Games. In M. E. Price & D. Dayan, eds., *Owning the Olympics: Narratives of the New China*. Ann Arbor: University of Michigan Press, pp. 185–209.

Collins, S. (2011). East Asian Olympic Desires: Identity on the Global Stage in the 1964 Tokyo, 1988 Seoul and 2008 Beijing Games. *The International Journal of the History of Sport*, 28(16), 2240–60.

Confucius Institute Headquarter/Hanban. (2006). *Confucius Institute Charter*, www.moe.gov.cn/srcsite/zsdwxxgk/200610/t20061001_62461.html.

Cook, S. (2020). *The Expansion of Chinese Communist Party Media Influence since 2017*, https://freedomhouse.org/report/special-report/2020/beijings-global-megaphone.

CPC News. (2019). Improve National Soft Power, Tell the China Story Well [提高国家软实力，讲好中国故事], http://theory.people.com.cn/n1/2019/0107/c40531-30507321.html.

Cull, N. J. (2008). The Public Diplomacy of the Modern Olympic Games and China's Soft Power Strategy. In M. E. Price & D. Dayan, eds., *Owning the Olympics: Narratives of the New China*. Ann Arbor: University of Michigan Press, pp. 117–44.

De Kloet, J., Chong, G. P. L., & Liu, W. (2008). The Beijing Olympics and the Art of Nation-State Maintenance. *China Aktuell – Journal of Contemporary Chinese Affairs*, 37(2), 5–35.

Dikötter, F. (1992). *The Discourse of Race in Modern China*. Stanford, CA: Stanford University Press.

Ding, S. (2010). Analyzing Rising Power from the Perspective of Soft Power: A New Look at China's Rise to the Status Quo Power. *Journal of Contemporary China*, 19(64), 255–72.

Dong, L. & Chapman, D. W. (2008). The Chinese Government Scholarship Program: An Effective Form of Foreign Assistance? *International Review of Education*, 54(2), 155–73.

Dynon, N. (2014). *Shanghai 2010 World Expo at Street Level: The Local Dimensions of a Public Diplomacy Spectacle*, https://uscpublicdiplomacy.org/blog/shanghai-2010-world-expo-street-level-local-dimensions-public-diplomacy-spectacle.

Economy, E. C. (2021). Podcast: Claudia Trevisan on China's Influence in Latin America, www.cfr.org/podcasts/podcast-claudia-trevisan-chinas-influence-latin-america.

Epstein, E. (2018). How China Infiltrated US Classrooms, www.politico .com/magazine/story/2018/01/16/how-china-infiltrated-us-classrooms-216327.

Fan, C. & Zou, C. (2013). "Chinese Language Heat" Rises in Many Countries in Central Asia, Confucius Institutes "Blooming Everywhere" [中亚多国兴起 "汉语热" 孔子学院 "遍地开花"], www.chinanews.com/hwjy/2013/09-18/ 5298370.shtml.

Farrow, R. & Farrow, M. (2007). The "Genocide Olympics," www.wsj.com/ articles/SB117505109799351409.

Fearon, T. & Rodrigues, U. M. (2019). The Dichotomy of China Global Television Network's News Coverage. *Pacific Journalism Review: Te Koakoa*, 25(1 & 2), 102–21.

Feng, E. (2018). China and the World: How Beijing Spreads the Message, www .ft.com/content/f5d00a86-3296-11e8-b5bf-23cb17fd1498.

Feng, E. (2019). China's Tech Giant Huawei Spans Much of the Globe Despite US Efforts to Ban It, www.npr.org/2019/10/24/759902041/chinas-tech-giant -huawei-spans-much-of-the-globe-despite-u-s-efforts-to-ban-it.

Feng, T. (2016). On Soft Power ["软实力"刍议]. *Wenhua Ruanshili Yanjiu*, 1 (1), 11–13.

Finley, C. J. & Xin X. (2010). Public Diplomacy Games: A Comparative Study of American and Japanese Responses to the Interplay of Nationalism, Ideology and Chinese Soft Power Strategies around the 2008 Beijing Olympics. *Sports in Society*, 13(5), 876–900.

Fudan University Media and Public Opinion Research Center. (2010). *Shanghai Citizens' Perception, Attitude and Evaluation of China's 2010 Shanghai World Expo* [上海市民对中国 *2010* 年上海世界博览会认知、态度及其 评价]. Cited in Cao, J. (2010). 95% of People Think the Expo Was a Big Success [九成五认为世博会圆满成功], https://epaper.gmw.cn/gmrb/html/ 2010-11/01/nw.D110000gmrb_20101101_3-03.htm.

Fulda, A. (2019). Chinese Propaganda Has No Place on Campus, *Foreign Policy*, https://foreignpolicy.com/2019/10/15/confucius-institute-chinese-propaganda-campus-communist-party-censorship/.

Gagliardone, I. (2013). China as a Persuader: CCTV Africa's First Steps in the African Mediasphere. *Ecquid Novi: African Journalism Studies*, 34(3), 25–40.

Gagliardone, I. & Pál, N. (2017). Freer but Not Free Enough? Chinese Journalists Finding Their Feet in Africa. *Journalism*, 18(8), 1049–63.

Geall, S. & Soutar, R. (2018). Chinese Media and Latin-America: "Borrowing a Boat" to Set Sail. *China Brief*, 18(12), https://jamestown.org/program/ chinese-media-and-latin-america-borrowing-a-boat-to-set-sail/#:~:text=%

E2%80%9CBorrowing%20a%20boat%20to%20go,is%20extending%20its %20reach%20into.

Gil, J. A. (2009). China's Confucius Institute Project: Language and Soft Power in World Politics. *Global Studies Journal*, 2(1), 59–72.

Gillespie, S. (2001). *South-South Transfer: A Study of Sino-African Exchanges*, New York: Routledge.

Global Times. (2010). African Cultural Ambassadors, www.globaltimes.cn/ content/591344.shtml.

Goldstein, J. (2018). Kenyans Say Chinese Investment Brings Racism and Discrimination, *New York Times*, www.nytimes.com/2018/10/15/world/ africa/kenya-china-racism.html.

Gong, T. (2007). On the Dimensions of Soft Power [论软权力的维度]. *Shijie Jingji yu Zhengzhi*, 9, 16–22. Cited in Li, M. (2008). China Debates Soft Power. *The Chinese Journal of International Politics*, 2(2), 287–308.

Graziani, S., Romano, A., & Zanier, V. (2017). The Case of Youth Exchanges and Interactions between the PRC and Italy in the 1950s. *Modern Asian Studies*, 51(1), 194–226.

Green-Riley, N. (2020). The State Department Labeled China's Confucius Programs a Bad Influence on US Students. What's the Story? *Washington Post*, www.washingtonpost.com/politics/2020/08/24/state-department-labeled-chinas-confucius-programs-bad-influence-us-students-whats-story/.

Guo, Q. (2016). Sinology and Cultural Soft Power [国学与文化软实力]. *Wenhua Ruanshili Yanjiu*, 1(1), 61–70.

Guo, Z. & Lye, L. F. (2011). *China's Television "Going Out" and the Dynamics of Media Competition within China*. Singapore: East Asian Institute, National University of Singapore. Cited in Zhao, Y. (2013). China's Quest for "Soft Power": Imperatives, Impediments and Irreconcilable Tensions? *Javnost – The Public*, 20(4), 17–29.

Han, B. (2015). Side Note of People in Beijing Celebrating Successful Bid for the Winter Olympics [首都群众庆祝申冬奥成功侧记], http://finance .sina.com.cn/roll/20150801/080122850800.shtml.

Han, Y. (2006). The Framework of the Strategy of Building China's Image under the Background of Globalization [全球化背景下的中国国家形象战略框架]. *Dangdai Shijie Yu Shehui Zhuyi* (1), 99–104.

Hartig, F. (2012). Confucius Institutes and the Rise of China. *Journal of Chinese Political Science / Association of Chinese Political Studies*, 17, 53–76.

Hartig, F. (2014). New Public Diplomacy Meets Old Public Diplomacy – the Case of China and Its Confucius Institutes. *New Global Studies; Berlin*, 8(3), 331–52.

Haugen, H. Ø. (2013). China's Recruitment of African University Students: Policy Efficacy and Unintended Outcomes. *Globalisation, Societies and Education*, 11(3), 315–34.

He, L. (2019). How China Is Closing the Soft Power Gap in Latin America, www.americasquarterly.org/article/how-china-is-closing-the-soft-power-gap-in-latin-america/.

He, W. (2021). Construct a Closer China-Africa Shared Future in Post-Pandemic Era [构建后疫情时代更紧密的中非命运共同体], https://news.gmw.cn/2021-01/03/content_34513185.htm.

Hsu, J. Y., Hildebrandt, T., & Hasmath, R. (2016). "Going Out" or Staying In? The Expansion of Chinese NGOs in Africa. *Development Policy Review*, 34(3), 423–39.

Hu, Z. & Ji, D. (2012). Ambiguities in Communicating with the World: The "Going-Out" Policy of China's Media and its Multilayered Contexts. *Chinese Journal of Communication*, 5(1), 32–7.

Hu, Z. & Wang, R. (2016). The Construction of Chinese Media Cultural Soft Power [中国传媒文化软实力的建构]. *Wenhua Ruanshili Yanjiu*, 1(2), 18–22.

Huang, J. & Ding, Z. (2010). Retrospection and Reflection on Studies of China's National Soft Power Construction [中国国家软实力建设路径研究的回顾与反思]. *Jiaoxue Yu Yanjiu* 11, 40–8.

Hubbert, J. (2017). Back to the Future: The Politics of Culture at the Shanghai Expo. *International Journal of Cultural Studies*, 20(1), 48–64.

Hubbert, J. (2019). *China in the World: An Anthropology of Confucius Institutes, Soft Power, and Globalization*. Honolulu: University of Hawai'i Press.

Hubbert, J. (2010). Spectacular Productions: Community and Commodity in the Beijing Olympics. *City and Society*, 22(1), 119–42.

Hubbert, J. (2014). The Darfur Olympics: Global Citizenship and the 2008 Beijing Olympic Games. *Positions*, 22(1), 203–36.

International Society for Chinese Language Teaching Secretariat. (2010). National Hanban/Confucius Institute Headquarter Publishes 2009 Annual Report [国家汉办/孔子学院总部发布 2009 年度报告]. *Shijie Hanyu Jiaoxue Xuehui Tongxun*, 2, 34.

Jardine, B. (2019). Why Are There Anti-China Protests in Central Asia? www.washingtonpost.com/politics/2019/10/16/why-are-there-anti-china-protests-central-asia/.

Jiang, F. & Zhang, N. (2019). Three Waves of International Communication in China (1978–2019) [中国对外传播的三次浪潮(1978–2019)]. *Quanqiu Chuanmei Xuekan*, 6(2), 39–58.

Jiang, Y. & Ye, J. (2009). Interpretation of Joseph Nye's "Soft Power" Concept [对约瑟夫奈软实力概念的解读]. *Zhengzhixue Yanjiu* 5, 114–24.

Jain, R. (2020). China's Strategic Foray into Higher Education: Goals and Motivations vis-à-vis Nepal. *Diplomacy & Statecraft*, 31(3), 534–56.

Jin, Z. & Shi, G. (2019). Confucius Institutes in Italy: Status Quo, Problems and Strategies [意大利孔子学院发展现状，问题与策略研究]. *Guoji Hanyu Jiaoxue Yanjiu*, 23(3), 12–18.

Keane, S. (2021). Huawei Ban Timeline: Chinese Company's Android Rival Is Coming to Phones and Tablets. Cnet. www.cnet.com/news/huawei-ban-timeline-chinese-company-android-rival-coming-phones-tablets/.

Kent, J. L. (2008). Faking Their Way to a Perfect Olympics, https://abcnews.go.com/International/China/story?id=5565191&page=1.

King, K. (2013). *China's Aid & Soft Power in Africa: The Case of Education and Training*. Woodbridge, Suffolk; Rochester, NY: Boydell & Brewer.

Klimeš, O. (2018). China's Cultural Soft Power: The Central Concept in the Early Xi Jinping Era (2012–2017). *AUC PHILOLOGICA* 4, 127–50.

Kluver, R. (2017). Chinese Culture in a Global Context: The Confucius Institute as a Geo-Cultural Force. In J. DeLisle & A. Goldstein, eds., *China's Global Engagement: Cooperation, Competition, and Influence in the 21st Century*. Washington, DC: Brookings Institution, pp. 389–416.

Kurlantzick, J. (2020). *Assessing China's Digital Silk Road: A Transformative Approach to Technology Financing or a Danger to Freedoms?* www.cfr.org/blog/assessing-chinas-digital-silk-road-transformative-approach-technology-financing-or-danger.

Lahtinen, A. (2015). China's Soft Power: Challenges of Confucianism and Confucius Institutes. *Journal of Comparative Asian Development*, 14(2), 200–26.

Latham, K. (2009). Media, the Olympics and the Search for the Real China: Special Section on the Beijing 2008 Olympics. *China Quarterly*, 197, 25–43.

Lau, J. (2021). International university students wait as China remains closed to them, *South China Morning Post*. https://www.scmp.com/news/china/article/3158455/international-university-students-wait-china-remains-closed-them.

Lau, J. (2020). China Moves to Smooth Relations with African Students, www.timeshighereducation.com/news/china-moves-smooth-relations-african-students.

Lau, S. (2021). China's Eastern Europe Strategy Gets the Cold Shoulder, www.politico.eu/article/china-xi-jinping-eastern-europe-trade-agriculture-strategy-gets-the-cold-shoulder/.

Lee, C. K. (2017). *The Specter of Global China: Politics, Labor, and Foreign Investment in Africa*, Chicago: University of Chicago Press.

Li, A. (2018). African Students in China: Research, Reality, and Reflection. *African Studies Quarterly*, 17(4), 5–44.

Li, J. & Tian, X. (2015). A Global Internationalization Experiment of Chinese Universities: Models, Experiences, Challenges and Prospects of Confucius Institutes' First Decade [中国大学国际化的一个全球试验—孔子学院十年之路的模式、经验与政策前瞻]. *Zhongguo Gaojiao Yanjiu*, 4, 37–43.

Li, M. (2008). China Debates Soft Power. *The Chinese Journal of International Politics*, 2(2), 287–308.

Li, M. ed. (2009). *Soft Power: China's Emerging Strategy in International Politics*. Lanham, MD: Lexington Books.

Li, S. & Tucker, G. R. (2013). A Survey of the US Confucius Institutes: Opportunities and Challenges in Promoting Chinese Language and Culture Education. *Journal of the Chinese Language Teachers Association*, 48 (1), 29–53.

Li, X. & Song, S. (2019). Current Situation, Problems, and Solutions of Admission Systems for International Students in China [来华留学生选拔制度的现状、问题及改善策略]. *Jiaoyu Xueshu Yuekan*, 3, 75–81.

Li, Y. W. (2013). Public Diplomacy Strategies of the 2008 Beijing Olympics and the 2012 London Olympics: A Comparative Study. *International Journal of the History of Sport*, 30(15), 1723–34, tandfonline.com/doi/abs/10.1080/09523367.790374

Liang, L. (2012). Going Live: News Innovations amid Constraints in the Chinese Coverage of the Iraq War. *Journalism*, 13(4), 450–66.

Lien, D., Oh, C. H., & Selmier, W. T. (2012). Confucius Institute Effects on China's Trade and FDI: Isn't It Delightful When Folks Afar Study Hanyu? *International Review of Economics & Finance*, 21(1), 147–55.

Lim, L. & Bergin, J. (2018). Inside China's audacious global propaganda campaign. *The Guardian*. www.theguardian.com/news/2018/dec/07/china-plan-for-global-media-dominance-propaganda-xi-jinping.

Liu, M. (2019). *2019* International Chinese Language Education Conference Concludes in Changsha [*2019* 年国际中文教育大会在长沙闭幕], www.chinanews.com/sh/2019/12-10/9030138.shtml.

Liu, X. (2019). China's Cultural Diplomacy: A Great Leap Outward with Chinese Characteristics? Multiple Comparative Case Studies of the Confucius Institutes. *Journal of Contemporary China*, 28(118), 646–61.

Liu, Y. (2017a). Discourse, the National Image, and China's Rise – The Discourse Construct of China's National Image [话语、国家形象与中国崛起–论中国国家形象的话语塑造]. *Lilun Yuekan*, 1, 161–7.

Liu, Y. (2017b). Hunan-Ethiopia Investment Cooperation Matchmaking Event Takes Places in Changsha, Xu Dazhe Gives a Speech [湖南-埃塞俄比亚投

资合作对接会长沙举行 许达哲致辞], https://hn.rednet.cn/c/2017/05/19/4299047.htm.

Ljunggren, D. (2020). Canada Has Effectively Moved to Block China's Huawei from 5G, but Can't Say So. *Reuters*, www.reuters.com/article/us-canada-huawei-analysis-idUSKBN25L26S.

Lu, G. (2007). Weak Cultural Soft Power Makes China Lose Advantages (in Competitions) – with a Discussion with Professor Yan Xuetong [文化实力弱让中国失分–与阎学通教授商榷]. *Shijixing*, 6, 45–6.

Lueck, T. L., Pipps, V. S., & Lin, Y. (2014). China's Soft Power: A *New York Times* Introduction of the Confucius Institute. *Howard Journal of Communications*, 25(3), 324–49.

Luo, J. (2019). Exchanges of Governance Experiences between China and Developing Countries: History, Theory and World Significance [中国与发展中国家的治国理政经验交流: 历史、理论与世界意义]. *Xiya Feizhou*, 4, 3–23.

Luo, J. (2017). Major Country Diplomacy with Chinese Characteristics: New Concepts, Strategy, and Characteristics] [中国特色大国外交: 新理念、新战略与新特色]. *Xiya Feizhou* 4, 28–49.

Luo, Y. (2013). Cultural Soft Power: Discourse Innovation Based on China's Practices [文化软实力: 基于中国实践的话语创新]. *Zhongguo Shehui Kexue* 1, 20–4.

Lovell, J. (2019). *Maoism: A Global History*. New York: Alfred A. Knopf.

Lynch, D. C. (2020). The End of China's Rise: Consequences for PRC Debate on Soft Power. In K. Edney, S. Rosen & & Y. Zhu, eds., *Soft Power with Chinese Characteristics: China's Campaign for Hearts and Minds*. London: Routledge, pp. 45–62.

Madrid-Morales, D. (2016). Why Are Chinese Media in Africa? Evidence from Three Decades of Xinhua's News Coverage of Africa. In X. Zhang, H. Wasserman, & W. Mano, eds., *China's Media and Soft Power in Africa: Promotion and Perceptions*. New York: Palgrave Macmillan, pp. 79–92.

Madrid-Morales, D. (2018). "Going out" – China in African media, https://africasacountry.com/2018/04/going-out-china-in-african-media.

Manzenreiter, W. (2010). The Beijing Games in the Western Imagination of China: The Weak Power of Soft Power. *Journal of Sport & Social Issues*, 34(1), 29–48.

Marsh, J. (2018). The Chinese Phone Giant That Beat Apple to Africa, www.cnn.com/2018/10/10/tech/tecno-phones-africa/index.html.

Marsh, V. (2017). Tiangao or Tianxia? The Ambiguities of CCTV's English-Language News for Africa. In D. K. Thusse, H. de Burgh, & A. Shi, eds., *China's Media Go Global*. Abingdon: Routledge, pp. 103–21.

Marsh, V. (2018). Re-Evaluating China's Global Media Expansion. *Westminster Papers in Communication and Culture*, 13(1), 143–6.

Mattern, J. B. (2005). Why "Soft Power" Isn't So Soft: Sociolinguistic Construction of Attraction in World Politics. *Millenium – Journal of International Studies*, 33(3), 583–612.

Maweu, J. M. (2016). Journalists' and Public Perceptions of the Politics of China's Soft Power in Kenya under the "Look East" Foreign Policy. In X. Zhang, H. Wasserman, & W. Mano, eds., *China's Media and Soft Power in Africa: Promotion and Perceptions*. New York: Palgrave Macmillan, pp. 123–34.

McCormick, A. (2019). Even if You Don't Think You Have a Relationship with China, China Has a Big Relationship with You. An Oral History of China's Foreign Press Training Programs, www.cjr.org/special_report/china-foreign-journalists-oral-history.php.

McIlroy, T. (2020). Review to Target Confucius Institute Deals, www.afr.com/politics/federal/review-to-target-confucius-institute-deals-20200828-p55qa7.

Meade, A. (2020). Nine Entertainment Newspapers Quit Carrying China Watch Supplement. *The Guardian*. www.theguardian.com/media/2020/dec/09/nine-entertainment-newspapers-quit-carrying-china-watch-supplement.

Men, H. (2007). Assessment Report of China's Soft Power (The Second Part) [中国软实力评估报告(下)]. *Guoji Guancha* 3, 37–46; 28.

Metzgar, E. T. (2016). Institutions of Higher Education as Public Diplomacy Tools: China-Based University Programs for the 21st Century. *Journal of Studies in International Education*, 20(3), 223–41.

Ministry of Education. (2017). *Zooming in on National Strategy, Providing Talent Support, the Work of Studying Abroad Achieves Significant Results* [聚焦国家战略 提供人才支撑 留学工作取得显著成绩], www.moe.gov.cn/jyb_xwfb/xw_fbh/moe_2069/xwfbh_2017 n/xwfb_170301/17030 1_sfcl/201 703/t20170301_297675.html.

Ministry of Education. (2018). *Notification about the Ministry of Education Promulgating "Quality Assurance for Higher Education of Foreign Students in China (Provisional)"* [教育部关于印发《来华留学生高等教育质量规范(试行)》的通知], www.moe.gov.cn/srcsite/A20/moe_850/201810/t20181012_351302.html.

Ministry of Science and Technology. (2020). *High-End Foreign Expert Recruitment Program Application (2020)* [高端外国专家引进计划申报书(2020)], www.wchscu.cn/staff/notice/50414.html.

Mohanmmed, O. (2015). A Chinese Media Company Is Taking Over East Africa's Booming Pay-TV Market, https://qz.com/africa/470166/a-chinese-media-company-is-taking-over-east-africas-booming-pay-tv-market/.

Morales, P. S. (2018). Could Chinese News Channels Have a Future in Latin America? *Westminster Papers in Communication and Culture*, 13(1), 60–80.

Muller, M. (2015). What Makes an Event a Mega Event? Definitions and Sizes. *Leisure Studies*, 34, 627–42.

Mycos. (2019). *2019 Chinese College Students Employment Report* [*2019 年中国大学生就业报告* (就业蓝皮书)]. Cited in Ye, H. (2019). Employment Bluebook: Class of 2018 College Graduates Employment Rate is 91.5% [就业蓝皮书: *2018* 届大学毕业生就业率为 *91.5%*], www.xinhuanet.com /2019-06/11/c_1210156279.htm.

National Association of Scholars. (2021). How Many Confucius Institutes Are in the United States? https://baijiahao.baidu.com/s?id=1636039285349 138315&wfr=spider&for=pc.

NBC News. (2008). Young Olympics Singing Star Didn't Really Sing. www.nbcnews.com/id/wbna26153578.

Nielsen. (2008). Beijing Olympics Draw Largest Ever Global TV Audience, www.nielsen.com/us/en/insights/article/2008/beijing-olympics-draw-largest-ever-global-tv-audience/.

Nye, J. S. (1990). Soft Power. *Foreign Policy*, 80, 153–71.

Nye, J. S. (1991). *Bound to Lead: The Changing Nature of American Power*. New York: Basic Books.

Nye, J. S. (2004). *Soft Power: The Means to Success in World Politics*. New York: Public Affairs.

Nye, J. S. (2009). Get Smart: Combining Hard and Soft Power. *Foreign Affairs*, 88(4), 160–3.

Office of Confucius Institute, Nanjing University. Chinese Directors [中方院长], https://confucius.nju.edu.cn/zfyz/list.htm.

Olander, E. C. (2020). 2020 in Review: The Impact of the "Guangzhou Incidents," https://chinaafricaproject.com/podcasts/2020-in-review-the-impact-of-the-guangzhou-incidents/.

Pagano, J. (2018). African Students, Encountering Racism at Top-Tier Chinese University, Raise Questions for China's Expanding Education Initiatives, https://medium.com/@jakepagano/african-students-encounter-institutional-racism-at-a-top-chinese-university-raising-urgent-cd8a6ee b1fa4.

Pan, C, Isakhan, B., & Nwokora, Z. (2020). Othering as Soft-Power Discursive Practice: *China Daily*'s Construction of Trump's America in the 2016 Presidential Election. *Politics*, 40(1), 54–69.

Pang, Z. (2005). The Connotation of China's Soft Power [中国软力量的内涵]. *Liaowang Xinwen Zhoukan* 45, 64.

People's Daily. (2020). China (Henan) – Switzerland Industrial Promotion Event Takes Place in Shanghai [中国(河南)–瑞士产业推介对接会在沪举行], www.sohu.com/a/430132210_114731.

Peterson, R. (2017). Outsourced to China: Confucius Institutes and Soft Power in American Higher Education, www.nas.org/reports/outsourced-to-china/full-report#Textbooks.

Pew Research Center. (2009). *Confidence in Obama Lifts US Image Around the World*, www.pewresearch.org/global/2009/07/23/chapter-3-rating-major-powers/.

Pew Research Center. (2011). *China Seen Overtaking US as Global Superpower*, www.pewresearch.org/global/2011/07/13/china-seen-overtaking-us-as-global-superpower/.

Price, M. E. (2008). Introduction. In M. E. Price & D. Dayan, eds., *Owning the Olympics: Narratives of the New China*. Ann Arbor: University of Michigan Press, pp. 1–14.

Procopio, M. (2015). The Effectiveness of Confucius Institutes as a Tool of China's Soft Power in South Africa. *African East-Asian Affairs* 2, 98–125.

Qing, K. G. & Shiffman, J. (2015). Beijing's Covert Radio Network Airs China-Friendly News across Washington, and the World, www.reuters.com/investigates/special-report/china-radio/.

Rawnsley, G. D. (2015). To Know Us Is to Love Us: Public Diplomacy and International Broadcasting in Contemporary Russia and China. *Politics*, 35(3–4), 273–86.

Repnikova, M. (2017). *Media Politics in China: Improvising Power Under Authoritarianism*, New York: Cambridge University Press.

Repnikova, M. & Fang, K. (2018). Authoritarian Participatory Persuasion 2.0: Netizens as Thought Work Collaborators in China. *Journal of Contemporary China*, 27(113), 763–79.

Roselle, L., Miskimmon, A., & O'Loughlin, B. (2014). Strategic Narrative: A New Means to Understand Soft Power. *Media, War & Conflict*, 7(1), 70–84.

Rosentiel, T. (2008). An Enthusiastic China Welcomes the Olympics, www.pewresearch.org/2008/08/05/an-enthusiastic-china-welcomes-the-olympics/.

RSF. (2018). China's Pursuit of a New World Media Order, https://rsf.org/sites/default/files/en_rapport_chine_web_final.pdf.

Sahlins, M. (2018). *Confucius Institute: Academic Malware and Cold Warfare*, www.insidehighered.com/views/2018/07/26/confucius-institutes-function-propaganda-arms-chinese-government-opinion.

Sanny, J. A. & Selormey, E. (2020). *Africans Regard China's Influence as Significant and Positive, but Slipping.* Afrobarometer 407, https://afrobarometer .org/sites/default/files/publications/Dispatches/ad407-chinas_perceived_influen ce_in_africa_decreases-afrobarometer_dispatch-14nov20.pdf.

Shayakhmetova, Z. (2018). Astana's Confucius Institute Promotes Cultural Ties, Launches Courses for Children, https://astanatimes.com/2018/05/astanas-confucius-institute-promotes-cultural-ties-launches-courses-for-children/.

Shen, Z. (2017). The Chinese Logic of the Construction of Cultural Power [文化强国建设的中国逻辑]. *Wenhua Ruanshili Yanjiu*, 2(2), 5–13; 2.

Shu, J. (2017). Reflections and Thoughts of Chinese Cultural Soft Power Studies [中国文化软实力研究的回顾与思考]. *Wenhua Ruanshili* 2, 33–9.

Shi, J. & Hu, H. (2019). 492,200 International Students from 196 Countries and Regions Came to China Last Year [*196 个国家和地区的 49.22 万名留学生去年来华留学*], www.xinhuanet.com/2019-06/03/c_1124578973.htm.

Silver, L., Devlin, K., & Huang, C. (2020). *Unfavorable Views of China Reach Historic Highs in Many Countries*, www.pewresearch.org/global/2020/10/06/unfavorable-views-of-china-reach-historic-highs-in-many-countries/.

Smith, B. (2008). Journalism and the Beijing Olympics: Liminality with Chinese Characteristics. In M. E. Price & D. Dayan, eds., *Owning the Olympics: Narratives of the New China*. Ann Arbor: University of Michigan Press, pp. 210–26.

Southern Metropolis Daily. (2020). Cuts to Financial Allocation of More than 60 Universities Exceeds Ten Billion Yuan, Budget of These Three Schools Were Cut the Most [*60 余高校财政拨款经费减少超百亿, 这三所大学被"砍"经费最多*], www.sohu.com/a/405796094_161795.

State Council. (2015). *Notification about the State Council Promulgating "Made in China 2025"* [国务院关于印发《中国制造 2025》的通知], www.gov.cn/zhengce/content/2015-05/19/content_9784.htm.

Sukumaran, T. (2019). Malaysia's May 13 Racial Riots: 50 Years on, They Couldn't Happen Again, Could They? www.scmp.com/week-asia/society/article/3009804/malaysias-may-13-racial-riots-50-years-they-couldnt-happen-again.

Sun, W. (2010a). Mission Impossible? Soft Power, Communication Capacity, and the Globalization of Chinese Media. *International Journal of Communication*, 4, 19–26.

Sun, W. (2010b). Motherland Calling: China's Rise and Diasporic Responses. *Cinema Journal*, 49(3), 126–30.

Sun, W. (2015). Slow Boat from China: Public Discourses behind the "Going Global" Media Policy. *International Journal of Cultural Policy*, 21(4), 400–18.

Tao, L. (2018). Japan Latest Country to Exclude Huawei, ZTE from 5G Roll-Out over Security Concerns. *South China Morning Post*, www.scmp.com/tech/tech-leaders-and-founders/article/2177194/japan-decides-exclude-huawei-zte-government.

The Associated Press. (2018). Young Olympics Singing Star Didn't Really Sing. www.nbcnews.com/id/wbna26153578.

The CPC Central Committee and The State Council. (2016). The CPC Central Committee and the State Council Issued the "Opinions on the Work of the Opening-Up of Education in the New Era" [中共中央办公厅、国务院办公厅印发《关于做好新时期教育对外开放工作的若干意见》], www.gov.cn/xinwen/2016-04/29/content_5069311.htm.

The Economist. (2018). China Is Spending Billions on Its Foreign-Language Media, www.economist.com/china/2018/06/14/china-is-spending-billions-on-its-foreign-language-media.

The Guardian. (2008). The Cost of the Beijing Olympics, www.theguardian.com/sport/2008/jul/28/olympicgames2008.china1.

The New York Times. (2007). Residents Refused to Make Way for Beijing Olympics, www.nytimes.com/2007/08/03/world/asia/03iht-beijing.1.6972501.html.

Tian, F. (2019). Why Do Foreign Students Differ So Much from Chinese Students When It Comes to Grades? [外国留学生与中国学生的成绩为何差那么多?], https://new.qq.com/omn/20190720/20190720A0PJ5V00.html.

Tong, S. (2008). To Improve the Cultural Soft Strength of the Nation: Connotation, Background and Task [提高国际文化软实力: 内涵、背景和任务]. *Mao Zedong Deng Xiaoping Lilun Yanjiu* 4, 1–8.

Torres, D. (2017). China's Soft Power Offensive, www.politico.eu/article/china-soft-power-offensive-confucius-institute-education/.

Umejei, E. (2018). Chinese Media in Africa: Between Promise and Reality. *African Journalism Studies*, 39(2), 104–20.

US Department of State. (2020). Briefing with Assistant Secretary for East Asian and Pacific Affairs David R. Stilwell and Acting Director of the Office of Foreign Missions Clifton C. Seagroves on Actions Taken to Counter PRC Influence Operations, https://2017-2021.state.gov/briefing-with-assistant-secretary-for-east-asian-and-pacific-affairs-david-r-stilwell-and-acting-director-of-the-office-of-foreign-missions-clifton-c-seagroves-on-actions-taken-to-counter-prc-i/index.html.

US Government Accountability Office. (2019). *Agreements Establishing Confucius Institutes at US Universities Are Similar, but Institutes Operations Vary*, www.gao.gov/assets/gao-19-278.pdf.

US Senate Permanent Subcommittee on Investigations. (2019). *China's Impact on the US Education System*, www.hsgac.senate.gov/imo/media/doc/PSI% 20Report%20China%27s%20Impact%20on%20the%20US%20Education %20System.pdf.

Varrall, M. (2020). *Behind the News: Inside China Global Television Network*, www.lowyinstitute.org/publications/behind-news-inside-china-global-televi sion-network#_edn70.

Wamanji, E. (2019). Wamanji: Lanuage and Culture Are Instruments for Expansion of Chinese Empire, www.kenyantribune.com/wamanji-language- and-culture-are-instruments-for-expansion-of-chinese-empire/.

Wan, J. (2015). Propaganda or Proper Journalism? China's Media Expansion in Africa, https://africanarguments.org/2015/08/propaganda-or-proper-journal ism-chinas-Media-expansion-in-africa/.

Wang, J. (2020). *Why Dubai World Expo Matters*, https://uscpublicdiplomacy .org/blog/why-dubai-world-expo-matters.

Wang, P. & Dang, Q. (2018). Latin American Confucius Institutes Joint Meeting Takes Place in Chili [拉美孔子学院联席会议在智利举行], www .xinhuanet.com/world/2018-09/08/c_1123399832.htm.

Wang, W. & Curdt-Christiansen, X. L. (2016). Teaching Chinese to International Students in China: Political Rhetoric and Ground Realities. *The Asia-Pacific Education*, 25(5–6), 723–34.

Wang, X. & Guo, S. (2012). Meaning of National Cultural Soft Power: Review of Opinions and Reflections [国家文化软实力之涵义: 观点综述与反思辨析]. *Xueshu Zongshu Yu Dongtai* 3, 156–60.

Wang, Y. (2008). Beijing Olympic Organizing Committee: The Interference and Disturbance of the Olympic Torch Relay by Very Few "Tibet Independence" Members Enjoy No Popular Support [北京奥组委: 极少数"藏独"分子干扰和破坏火炬传递不得人心], http://news.sina.com.cn/c/2008-04-08/ 074013701274s.shtml.

Wang, Y. (2016). The Paradox of Soft Power and Its Chinese Surpass [论软实力悖论及其中国超越]. *Wenhua Ruanshili Yanjiu*, 1(2), 9–17.

Wang, Y. (2018). Chinese Characteristics of Cultural Soft Power [文化软实力的中国特性]. *Wenhua Ruanshili Yanjiu*, 3(2), 23–9.

Wang, Z. (2010). China Pavilion "Watershed of Chinese Architecture," www .chinadaily.com.cn/china/2010expo/2010-08/19/content_11174508.htm.

Wasserman, H. (2012). China in South Africa: Media Responses to a Developing Relationship. *Chinese Journal of Communication*, 5(3), 336–54.

Waterson, J. & Jones, S. D. (2020). *Daily Telegraph Stops Publishing Section Paid for by China. The Guardian*, www.theguardian.com/media/2020/apr/14/ daily-telegraph-stops-publishing-section-paid-for-by-china.

Watts, J. (2008). China Faked Footprints of Fire Coverage in Olympics Opening Ceremony, *The Guardian,* www.theguardian.com/sport/2008/aug/11/olympics2008.china.

Weibo Hashtag "2022 Winter Olympic." #2022 Winter Olympic# [#2022 冬季奥运会#], https://s.weibo.com/weibo?q=%232022%E5%86%AC%E5%AD%A3%E5%A5%A5%E8%BF%90%E4%BC%9A%23.

Wen, Z. (2013). Reflections on the Rapid Growth of Overseas Students in China [对来华留学生人数迅速增长的思考]. *Hanshan Shifan Xueyuan Xuebao* 2, 95–9.

Wheeler, A. (2014). Cultural Diplomacy, Language Planning, and the Case of the University of Nairobi Confucius Institute. *Journal of Asian and African Studies*, 49(1), 49–63.

Workneh, T. W. (2016). Chinese Multinationals in the Ethiopian Telecommu-nications Sector. *Communication, Culture and Critique*, 9(1), 126–47.

Xia, P., Wei, Z., Li, J., Cai, G., Zhao, Y., Chen, W., Hua, Y., Yuan, L., & Ren, J. (2020). "Chinese Language Heat" Continues to Warm up, Confucius Institutes Boosts the Development of International Chinese Language Education [*"汉语热"持续升温 孔子学院助力国际中文教育发展*], www.xinhuanet.com/world/2020-06/13/c_1126110341.htm.

Xiamen University. 2019 *Confucius Institute Annual Report* [*2019年孔子学院年度报告*], https://ocia.xmu.edu.cn/info/1045/8729.htm.

Xie, W. (2017). Chinese NGOs Exert Increasing Influence in Africa, www.globaltimes.cn/content/1058366.shtml.

Xinhua News Agency. (2010). Hu Jintao's Speech at the Summary and Commendation Conference of 2010 Shanghai World Expo [胡锦涛在*2010*年上海世博会总结表彰大会上的讲话], www.gov.cn/ldhd/2010-12/27/content_1773855.htm.

Xinhua News Agency. (2016). Xi Jinping: Persist on the Right Direction and Innovate the Methods, Improve the Dissemination and Guiding Force of News and Public Opinion [习近平: 坚持正确方向 创新方法手段 提高新闻舆论传播力引导力], www.xinhuanet.com//politics/2016-02/19/c_1118102868.htm.

Xinhua News Agency. (2017). Chinese Journalists Encouraged to Tell Stories to World, www.xinhuanet.com/english/2017-11/09/c_136740332.htm.

Xinhua News Agency. (2018). Xi Jinping's Keynote Speech at the 2018 FOCAC Beijing Summit (Full Text) [习近平在*2018*年中非合作论坛北京峰会开幕式上的主旨讲话*(全文)*], www.xinhuanet.com/world/2018-09/03/c_1123373881.htm.

Xinhua News Agency (2019). Confucius Institutes Opened in Eight Countries for the First Time [八个国家首次设立孔子学院], www.xinhuanet.com/politics/2019-12/10/c_1125331495.htm.

Xu, J. & Li, H. (2013). *Xu Lin: Strengthen Localization Building and Push Forward the Sustainable Development of Confucius Institutes* [许琳: 加强本土化建设 推动孔子学院持续发展], http://world.people.com.cn/n/2013/0529/c157278-21663329.html.

Xu, L. & Bao, L. (2019). Supply of Chinese Teachers for Confucius Institutes: Current Situation, Dilemma and Solution [孔子学院师资供给: 现状, 困境与变革]. *Zhejiang Shifan Daxue Xuebao (Shehui Kexue Ban)*, 44(3), 56–61.

Xu, S. & Qin, B. (2018). One Should Also Pursue Quality When Introducing Foreign Students, Avoid People Like "Gao Yanei Who Goof Off" [徐实、秦博: 引进留学生也要追求质量, 避免 "高衙内" 们浑水摸鱼], www.guancha.cn/xushi/2018_05_23_457623_s.shtml.

Xu, W. (2013). The Dilemma and Solution of the Advanced Culture Transmission under the Background of Globalization [全球化背景下当代中国文化传播的困境与出路]. *Shandong Daxue Xuebao (Zhexue Shehui Kexueban)* 4, 96–103.

Xu, Z. (2014). The Difficult Position and Resolution on Speaking Chinese Good Stories [讲好中国故事的现实困难与破解之策]. *Shehui Zhuyi Yanjiu*, 215(3), 20–6.

Yan, H. (2020). Experience and Inspiration from "Russia Today" Rebuilding National Image ["今日俄罗斯"重塑国家形象的经验与启示]. *Qingnian Jizhe* 33, 99–100.

Yan, X. (2007). The Core of Soft Power Is Political Power [软实力的核心是政治实力]. *Shijixing*, 6, 42–3.

Yan, X. & Xu, J. (2008). Comparison between Chinese Soft Power and US Soft Power [中美软实力比较]. *Xiandai Guoji Guanxi* 1, 24–9.

Yan, X. & Zhao, K. (2016). Promote Chinese Fine Traditional Culture, Enhancing National Cultural Soft Power [弘扬中华传统文化 增强国家文化软实力]. *Wenhua Ruanshili* 2, 46–51.

Yang, J. (2010). *Yang Jiechi Discusses World Expo Diplomacy: A New Start for China's Diplomacy* [杨洁篪谈世博外交: 中国外交的新起点], www.fmprc.gov.cn/web/gjhdq_676201/gjhdqzz_681964/lhg_683070/zyjh_683080/t736641.shtml.

Yang, J. & Zhang, Y. (2019). First China-Africa Trade Expo Is Fruitful [第一届中国-非洲经贸博览会成果丰硕], www.xinhuanet.com/fortune/2019-06/29/c_1124688926.htm.

Yang, R. (2007). China's Soft Power Projection in Higher Education. *International Higher Education*, 46, 24–5.

Yang, R. (2010). Soft Power and Higher Education: An Examination of China's Confucius Institutes. *Globalisation, Societies and Education*, 8(2), 235–45.

Yang, R. & Xie, M. (2015). Leaning Toward the Centers: International Networking at China's Five C9 League Universities. *Frontiers of Education in China*, 10(1), 66–90. Cited in Metzgar, E. T. (2016). Institutions of Higher Education as Public Diplomacy Tools: China-Based University Programs for the 21st Century. *Journal of Studies in International Education*, 20(3), 223–41.

Yang Wei, Confucius Institute Forum, Chinese International Education Foundation, https://cief.org.cn/z1.

Yao, X. (2007). Communication Methods of Public Relations and China's Soft Power Building [公共关系的传播手段与中国软实力建构]. *Xinwen Qianshao,* 7, 93–4. Cited in Li, M. (2008). China Debates Soft Power. *The Chinese Journal of International Politics*, 2(2), 287–308.

Yardley, J. (2008). Dissident's Arrest Hints at Olympic Crackdown, *New York Times,* www.nytimes.com/2008/01/30/world/asia/30dissident.html.

Ye, H. (2019). Employment Bluebook: Class of 2018 College Graduates Employment Rate is 91.5% [就业蓝皮书: *2018* 届大学毕业生就业率为 *91.5%*], www.xinhuanet.com/2019-06/11/c_1210156279.htm.

Ye, P. & Albornoz, L. A. (2018). Chinese Media "Going Out" in Spanish Speaking Countries: The Case of CGTN-Espanol. *Westminster Papers in Communication and Culture*, 13(1), 81–97.

Yu, K. & Zhuang, J. (2004). Hot Topic and Cold Analysis (Thirty Four) – The Dialogue between Beijing Consensus and the China Development Model [热话题与冷思考(三十四)—关于 '北京共识'与中国发展模式的会话]. *Dangdai Shijie Yu Shehui Zhuyi* 5, 4–9.

Zhan, C. & Lu, M. (2019). The Predicament and Optimization of Teaching Chinese to Speakers of Other Languages in Confucius Institute [孔子学院汉语国际教育的困境与优化分析]. *Xiandai Jiaoyu Luncong*, 230(6), 60–8.

Zhang, G. (2015). Cultural Soft Power Research [文化软实力研究]. *Zhongguo Gaoxiao Shehui Kexue* 1, 42–5.

Zhang, X. (2013). How Ready Is China for a China-Style World Order? China's State Media Discourse under Construction. *Ecquid Novi: African Journalism Studies*, 34(3), 79–101.

Zhang, Y. (2014). Understand China's Media in Africa from the Perspective of Constructive Journalism. Paper presented at the international conference, China and Africa, Communication and Diplomacy. Chr. Michelsen Institute and Chinese Academy of Social Sciences, 10–11 September, Beijing, www.cmi.no/file/2922-.pdf

Zhang, Y. & Matingwina, S. (2016). A New Representation of Africa? The Use of Constructive Journalism in the Narration of Ebola by *China Daily* and the BBC. *African Journalism Studies*, 37(3), 19–40.

Zhang, Y. & Mwangi, J. M. (2016). A Perception Study on China's Media Engagement in Kenya: From Media Presence to Power Influence? *Chinese Journal of Communication*, 9(1), 71–80.

Zhang, Z. (2018). Xi Jinping's "Beijing Time" of FOCAC [习近平的中非合作论坛"北京时间"], www.chinanews.com/gn/2018/09-05/8618771.shtml.

Zhao, K. (2005). Hard Diplomacy, Soft Landing: On the Formation and Consequences of the New Thought of China's Diplomacy [硬外交 软着陆: 试论中国外交新思维的形成与影响]. *Guoji Guancha* 5, 27–34.

Zhao, K. (2014). Problems and Mindset of Chinese Cultural Diplomacy [中国文化外交的问题与思路]. *Gonggong Waijiao Jikan* 2, 19–25; 125.

Zhao, L. (2007). Understanding Three Dimensions of Chinese Soft Power: Cultural Diplomacy, Multilateral Diplomacy and Foreign Aid Policies [理解中国软实力的三个维度:文化外交, 多边外交, 对外援助政策]. *Shehui Kexue Luntan* 5, 150–7.

Zhao, L. (2017). Violation of Laws by Chinese Citizens Overseas and "Diplomatic Protection" [中国公民在海外违法犯罪与 '领事保护'], www.xinhuanet.com/world/2017-07/13/c_129653626.htm.

Zhao, L. (2019). Group Portrait of International Students in China: Where From, What to Study, Whose Money Are They Spending? [来华留学生群像:从哪来, 学什么, 花谁的钱?], www.thepaper.cn/newsDetail_forward_4094168.

Zhao, X. (2018). "The Flower of Chinese Language" Blooms in Africa [*"汉语之花"绽放非洲*], http://world.people.com.cn/n1/2018/0831/c1002-30262924.html.

Zhao, Y. (2008). *Communication in China: Political Economy, Power, and Conflict*, Lanham, MD: Rowman & Littlefield.

Zhao, Y. (2013). China's Quest for "Soft Power": Imperatives, Impediments and Irreconcilable Tensions? *Javnost – The Public*, 20(4), 17–29.

Zheng, Y. & Zhang, C. (2007). Soft Power in International Politics and the Implications for China [国际政治中的软力量以及对中国软力量的观察]. *Shijie Jingji Yu Zheng Zhi* 7, 6–12; 3.

Zhong, Y. (2021). CCPCC National Committee Member Gao Yanming: Suggestions to Optimize the Policy for Foreign Students in China [全国政协委员高彦明: 建议优化外国来华留学生政策], https://m.thepaper.cn/newsDetail_forward_11572058.

Zou, S. (2018). Localisation between Negotiating Forces: A Case Study of a Chinese Radio Station in the United States. *Westminster Papers in Communication and Culture*, 13(1), 1–16.

Acknowledgement

I would like to thank Professor Ching Kwan Lee for her guidance and editorial comments on this Element, as well as the two anonymous reviewers for insightful suggestions and critiques. I would also like to thank Wendy Weile Zhou, Luwen, Wing Kuang and Kristy Lam for their invaluable research assistance, as well as the Wilson Center and Georgia State University for the research funding support that was critical to completing this project.

Cambridge Elements

Global China

Ching Kwan Lee
University of California-Los Angeles

Ching Kwan Lee is a professor of sociology at the University of California-Los Angeles. Her scholarly interests include political sociology, popular protests, labor, development, political economy, comparative ethnography, China, Hong Kong, East Asia and the Global South. She is the author of three multiple award-winning monographs on contemporary China: Gender and the South China Miracle: Two Worlds of Factory Women (1998), Against the Law: Labor Protests in China's Rustbelt and Sunbelt (2007), and The Specter of Global China: Politics, Labor and Foreign Investment in Africa (2017). Her co-edited volumes include Take Back Our Future: an Eventful Sociology of Hong Kong's Umbrella Movement (2019) and The Social Question in the 21st Century: A Global View (2019).

About the Series

The Cambridge Elements series Global China showcases thematic, region- or country-specific studies on China's multifaceted global engagements and impacts. Each title, written by a leading scholar of the subject matter at hand, combines a succinct, comprehensive and up-to-date overview of the debates in the scholarly literature with original analysis and a clear argument. Featuring cutting edge scholarship on arguably one of the most important and controversial developments in the 21st century, the Global China Elements series will advance a new direction of China scholarship that expands China Studies beyond China's territorial boundaries.

Cambridge Elements ☰

Global China

Elements in the series

Chinese Soft Power
Maria Repnikova

A full series listing is available at: www.cambridge.org/EGLC

Printed in the United States
by Baker & Taylor Publisher Services